Learning from Experience
Empowerment or Incorporation?

Wilma Fraser

*Is it possible that we practitioners may also be
unwitting agents of the very oppression or limitations
we seek to transcend by our good practice?*
(Mulligan and Griffin, Empowerment through
Experiential Learning, 1992)

NIACE
THE NATIONAL ORGANISATION
FOR ADULT LEARNING

Published by the National Institute of Adult
Continuing Education (England and Wales)
21 De Montfort Street, Leicester LE1 7GE
Company registration no. 2603322
Charity registration no. 1002775

First published 1995
Reprinted 1996

Cataloguing in Publication Data
A CIP record for this title is available from the British
Library

ISBN 1 872941 60 5

Printed and bound in Great Britain by Antony Rowe
Ltd, Chippenham
Printed on acid-free paper

Contents

DEDICATION

To my parents Bel and Greg Fraser. For their Scottish belief in the value of education, and for everything else besides ... with love.

Preface and Acknowledgements

Most educational practitioners, whether in the field of adult, further or higher education, have by now at least a nodding acquaintance with the work which has been undertaken in the area of accrediting or assessing prior learning (APL). APL's importance lies in having legitimised the inclusion of prior learning within assessment procedures across the spectrum of vocational and non-vocational certificating bodies.

In other words, the principle of including prior learning – whether towards the awarding of, for example, National Vocational Qualifications (NVQs), Business and Technician Education Council (BTEC) or Royal Society of Arts (RSA) diplomas, or in granting access to, or advanced standing within, higher education (HE) – has now been generally accepted as a means of acknowledging greater individual potential by valuing the importance of diverse sources of learning and the competences to be derived from them.

Broader-based facilities also abound. A number of providers, including Goldsmiths' College (University of London), the Workers' Educational Association (WEA) and the Open University (OU), have developed programmes under the general heading of 'Making Experience Count' (MEC). These concentrate less on specific and directed outcomes, whether vocational or educational, and instead provide a space in which participants reflect on the learning gained from their experiences and their current situations. They may then take stock of their needs and aspirations and decide upon possible next steps.

Some of these broader-based programmes have sought recognition from their local Open College Network (OCN). In these cases, participants may submit a portfolio of their learning 'outcomes' for external verification and accreditation. But because the learning outcomes within the MEC approach are not specifically tied to the competence requirements of a receiving institution or vocational assessor, there is theoretically greater scope for drawing upon learning gained from a broader range of experience.

This is why a number of practitioners within the field argue for a distinction between APL and APEL – the Assessment or Accreditation of Prior *Experiential* Learning. They contend that APEL preceded APL as a means of valuing the diversity of individual experience and included both formal and informal sources of learning. Increasingly, APL has restricted the types of learning and experience which may be utilised because its formalisation within certification procedures has demanded a greater systemic fit between the relevant competences of the individual and the specific requirements of the awarding body, employer or institution. Thus, much of the potential for valuing the range of individual experience, and finding creative outlets for its expression, is being eroded as market forces increasingly hold sway over issues of vocational and educational relevance and, by extension, of personal and social value.

In 1991, the WEA South Eastern District was funded by the WEA national organisation to run a series of six experiential learning courses entitled Making Your Experience Count and falling within the potentially broader APEL category. At one level, the learning gained from facilitating these courses justified our holding to this distinction between APEL and APL. But as the work progressed it became apparent that the very notion of 'counting experience' reveals a complexity that reaches far beyond the easy polarisation that such a distinction suggests. Indeed, the rhetoric surrounding AP(E)L's potential as an instrument for greater individual fulfilment all too often masks what is actually its incorporation within a restrictive societal conformity.

The questions that this book raises are not confined to the area of prior learning. Its concerns are the dilemmas, contradictions and debates around the current paradigmatic shifts within our definitions of – and practices within – the educational field. Whether or not we retain a distinction between vocational and liberal provision, wherever we place ourselves along the education/training faultline, we must still address the fundamental issues relating to means and purpose.

Apparently it is an historical truism that each generation claims that it is is witnessing the greatest rate of change that has ever been known. I can only attest to my own experiences and echo those of colleagues and friends who have repeated that claim many times during the last few years. In the race to keep up to date with government initiatives, funding changes and the resultant restructuring of all post-16 education (leaving aside changes within the primary and secondary sectors), we may be forgiven for not taking enough time to reflect upon the implications of one of the most invidious statements of the last 10 years. If 'there is no such thing as society', then 'experience' will never count except as an excuse for trumpeting individualism and a means to personal advancement for the few.

This book addresses practitioners across the board and urges a return to an educational ethos which embraces collective responsibility and works towards social change.

Acknowledgements

At each stage of the process of this book since its inception over two and a half years ago its progress has been sustained by the support and encouragement of friends, colleagues, acquaintances, chance conversations and in-depth analyses. To put it quite simply, it would not have been written without the help of the following. My grateful thanks to all.

Cathy Hull, for introducing me to MEC and to its potential, and for reading the first draft; Vernon Hull, our District Secretary, for encouraging MEC's development within our region; Trish Jolly, Sharon Kerrison, Carole Smith at the office for their continued good humour in the face of my total inability to come to terms with twentieth-century technology; and to Lesley Stiles, Senior Administrator, for her unfailing stoicism and equanimity no matter what impossible demand I make. Thanks too to my colleagues and friends in the field: to Jill Britcher for that particular quotation and many conversations, and to Sheila

Mathieson for sharing WEA 'highs and lows' with me over the past eight years.

Other friends old and new have played their part. I am grateful to Sheryl Anderson, Fran Bekhechi, Agnes Cardinal, Jenny Cross (for trying pastures new), Tony Chiva, Judy Colley (for her very timely encouragement), Sue Forward (for knowing exactly what I meant), Dorothy Goldman (for, among other things, 'the ticket'), Stan Graham, Patty Key and Stephen Kirby (old hands both), Katalin Lanczi (for her long-term patience), Melanie Lewin (for her reappearance – changed yet the same), Carol Lewis (for continuity; unchanged), Heather Malcolm (for beginning again), Fiona Roberts (for a totally different perspective), Penny Rose (for a similar one), Val Stirrup (for still believing) and Rosie Williams (for ensuring distance made no difference). Heartfelt thanks to Betty Choudhury, Ann Harrison, Linda Kushner, Joy Pascoe, for sharing your journeys with me and for 'being there', and to Joy for reading chapters in the early hours. And telling me not to start a sentence with 'And'. Especial thanks are also due to Linden West (for reading the first draft and sharing the struggle for 'a voice'), to David Alfred (friend, colleague and voluntary editor, who has suffered my idiosyncratic punctuation, and shone a critical beacon through the fog) and to Christopher Feeney (the 'official' editor at NIACE, who has supported the project from beginning to end with warmth, encouragement and generosity of spirit).

Finally, I must pay tribute to the courage of the students on our courses, who must remain anonymous, and to the hard work and commitment of the tutors whose names appear in the book. Thank you all for making this experience count.

Introduction

Private Selves and Public Expressions: A Question of Relevance

I wonder what it is that makes it so difficult for some people to commit themselves to paper? Friends and colleagues have assured me that the process of writing a book is painful and frustrating and demands rewrite after rewrite in the struggle to say something worthwhile. Well, this is the seventh draft of the Introduction and my struggle goes on. But what strikes me particularly about the acute anxiety that this project is causing is how the nature of my tears and frustrations differs from the usual degree of stress I feel when engaged in any other form of written work.

Reports, reviews, papers and programmes are usually dispatched with what in hindsight I can only regard as relative ease. The levels of anxiety remain in direct proportion to the time available for the exercise and my assumptions about the expectations of the different kinds of audiences I should be addressing. A report demands a different kind of language from that required by a review; recommendations and evaluations march to slightly dissimilar beats. In other words, there are frameworks or registers appropriate to the particular discursive activities within which we are engaged. And the success of our endeavours is largely determined by the extent to which our work conforms to the requirements these constructions demand of us.

If this were an academic treatise about the history and implications of our involvement in Making Experience Count (MEC) programmes, its relevance to the debate would be measured both by the language I adopted and the extent to which I incorporated and broadened the existing level of intellectual knowledge within the field of experiential learning. Indeed, the familiar academic signposts marked my progress throughout the first few drafts of the early chapters to the book. But the more I wrote, the more I realised that in straining after academic credibility I was moving further and further away from the complexities and contradictions that the MEC process entailed. The constructions available to us in the academic realm enable us to analyse a literary text or rationalise points of difference and similarity among diverse ideological viewpoints. They do not lend themselves so easily to areas of experience which are not already articulated in relation to recognisable 'subjects' or bodies of knowledge.

Making Experience Count courses are a form of APEL provision. The Assessment of Prior Experiential Learning, as the name indicates, utilises the learning gained from experience. Thus the subject matter of the programme is the student herself and the process of the programme involves articulating the relationship between the student and the wealth of experiences which have informed her interaction with the world.

The problematic nature of the 'self' does, of course, form the basis of many academic disciplines, philosophy and psychology being the most obvious. What I am trying to address here is the disjunction between public discourse and private experience and the particular modes of enquiry which are appropriate to each. For what strikes me so forcibly about my own fears in translating my thoughts and experiences into the public realm is the similarity between my process in writing this and that of the students on our courses.

The key to the heart of the MEC/APEL endeavour is the reflective process which will open the door to the learning derived from experience. The underlying assumption is of the self as a 'narrator' who can recollect experience and turn it into learning. 'Learning' is understood as a process which operates in any number of formal or informal situations. It is not restricted to scholastic or vocational environments but includes the learning gained from the myriad quotidian experiences we all encounter as we perform the various roles our social obligations demand of us. The intention of the MEC programme is to facilitate understanding and thence 'ownership' of the learning process, which will lead, in turn, to enhanced self-esteem and increased self-confidence. The process is in accord with one of the key tenets of the andragogical approach to learning, which is that 'adults are what they have done' (see Chapter 1). And this approach is reflected in the numerous publications offering lesson plans and programme notes to facilitate the reclamation process.

Many students regard that process as an end in itself, for the programme is seen as providing a diagnostic space in which adults may explore their prior experiences in a safe and non-judgemental environment, extricate the learning gained and utilise that learning according to the nature of their own goals and aspirations. At this level we can applaud the liberatory potential that MEC offers:

> *I thought I was just a housewife but this course has made me value just how much my caring and nurturing entails. I feel better about myself.*

The tutors on our project all attested to the numbers of students who claimed that the process had changed their lives.

I would never wish to decry the experience of individual empowerment that MEC courses can offer, yet deeper reflection brought home to me MEC/APEL's fundamental paradox. As long as recognition of the individual's learning process remains within the heart and mind of the student concerned, we can encourage the journey of discovery and applaud the outcome of increased self-esteem. But when students seek others' acknowledgement of the relevance of their new-found learning to, for example, vocational or educational requirements, they must articulate that learning in a manner which will meet the approval of an external reader – and assessor. Private concerns have now become a matter for public adjudication.

Where then is the problem with this? If 'adults are what they have done' then we should welcome the broadening of perspective which encourages recognition of hitherto unsung achievements and paves the way for access to greater opportunity. This was certainly my heartfelt belief when we began the MEC project.

Few would deny that the path to academic success has always been a narrow one; its turnstile, until very recently, lost to the majority in the forests of 'Unsuitability' and 'Impenetrability'. Equally, very few could deny that working patterns and practices, including unemployment and underemployment, have consistently failed to maximise human potential and encourage creative growth and expression. It is hardly surprising therefore that educationalists and vocationalists would applaud government initiatives to increase access and opportunity by accepting and thereby legitimising the inclusion of prior learning across the spectrum of vocational and non-vocational certificating bodies.

However, theory and practice rarely walk hand-in-hand. As I argue below and in the following chapters, my work (and that of many of my fellow tutors) with Making Experience Count programmes has laid bare the muddle, inconsistency and contradiction at the heart of these endeavours. On the one hand we argued for the space in which students may explore their potential and thence exercise greater control over their lives. On the other hand, we became all too aware of the glibness of the term 'adults are what they have done' because it is predicated upon a model of individualistic achievement which fails to address either social inequalities or the sheer irrationality so often at the heart of our humanity. The 'thousand natural shocks' also include the lessons learned, sometimes much more painfully and tragically, from experiences that we are subject to as members of different cultural, economic and gendered environments.

APEL assumes that competences learned in one sphere can be utilised and applied in a number of different contexts. But how realistic is this for students who fall within that broad classification 'the disadvantaged'? For those at the margins of political, economic and social power, the notion that they 'are what they have done' sounds more like a slap in the face than a term of encouragement; and we are all powerfully reminded that there are far greater barriers to opportunity and fulfilment than simply the acknowledgement of individual potential.

The MEC/APEL process further assumes a coherent and unified subject, 'I', who can reflect on experience, extricate the learning gained and use that learning as a means towards greater self-esteem; usually by translating the relevance of the learning to vocational or educational requirements. But this begs three basic questions:

- the concept of a unified subject enjoying equality of opportunity
- the concept of 'experience' as coherent, consistent and a site for rational intellectual excavation
- parity between learning gained in one arena and the skills and competences demanded by another.

Each of these issues is dealt with in greater detail in the course of the book. At this stage, I shall just note in general terms that the act of articulating the MEC/APEL process goes to the root of what constitutes the relationship between the private and public spheres. And any form of assessment, formal or informal, reveals the extent to which those spheres are constructed. For readers unfamiliar with constructionist debates, Norquay's (1990) explanation serves as a useful approach to the themes which follow:

> Both feminists and poststructuralists have suggested that identity is multiple, shifting and contradictory. Individuals have several subject positions from which they engage with the social historical contexts in which they live their lives (my emphasis).

As I noted at the beginning of this Introduction, I could not adopt a purely academic approach and feel I was doing justice to the contradictory nature of experiences that work with MEC entailed. Far from positing a consistent argument with a set of propositions leading to a logical conclusion, I found myself thrown back time and again into the welter of personal doubts and checks that mocked my endeavours. I was trying to reflect upon the experiences encountered in working with MEC, extricate the learning gained and articulate it in a manner which would fit with the conventional form of such written accounts. There are tried and tested formulas for this procedure; 'too much emotion' is frowned upon, anecdotes should be kept to a minimum, the narrative must proceed in an orderly fashion and be contained within the appropriate register. It will then find favour with the audience for which it is intended because it will be recognised as residing within the limits of their particular discourse. Materials, or experiences, which do not 'fit' must be eschewed in favour of clarity and consistency of purpose – their inclusion would render the project irrelevant, indulgent and cast severe doubt upon the competence and credibility of the writer.

In other words, certain experiences and modes of expression are acceptable; others are not. And this is true whether the arena is educational publishing or the shop floor. All modes of social engagement are regulated by discourses which, in turn, reflect the relative powers and correspondent 'equalities' measured out by cultural, political and socio-economic interests.

MEC/APEL courses are no exception. Whether we are talking about individuals at the first stage of private recollection and reflection or at the point where they seek public recognition for the value of their experiences, social or *regulatory practices* both inform and construct each step of the way. For we organise our lives according to narrative structures of greater or lesser effectiveness, which, in turn, depend upon our relative distance from society's loci of control. The stories that we tell about our selves and the sense that we make of our lives reflects the ways that these lives are constructed in relation to the powers that operate in our society. The extent to which we self-censor our experiences, 'select' the most 'relevant' and 'choose' the arenas where we can utilise the learning gained reveals the nature of those regulatory practices, if not always their goal and purpose. To put it crudely, the process tells us who, or what, is pulling the strings.

This is why Making Experience Count is a double-edged sword. It operates at the margins between our private and our public selves because it intervenes at the sites of self-disclosure, selection, relevance and control. In begging the question 'count towards what?' it can either 'cut the ties that bind' or sever our connection to perhaps the most creative parts of our selves because they are not 'relevant'.

But these are lessons learned in hindsight. This book is the story of the process that illuminated these, and related, conclusions. It tells the story of a project run by a team of tutors in the WEA South Eastern District, in a manner consistent with the requirements of narrative structure. The beginning and middle are succeeded in appropriate and Aristotelian fashion with a closure which rounds off the argument and completes the process. But it is also a 'portfolio'; submerged in our experiences we seek to extricate the learning gained and translate it for your adjudication.

APEL or APL?

I have already explained that our MEC courses are generally regarded as an extension of APEL provision (the assessment, or accreditation, of prior experiential learning). And in our WEA District we still retain a clear distinction between APEL and APL (the accreditation of prior learning). Many practitioners disagree, arguing that latterly, especially, 'APL' functions as the generic term and includes 'APEL' within its remit.

This view is theoretically true, but my concern is that current implementation of APL is increasingly reflective of a reductionist and outcome-oriented approach. In pursuit of the 'learning product' we are in danger of sacrificing the creative and critical process which should be at the heart of the educational endeavour. This is not to denigrate the work of many colleagues in the field who are striving to retain the potential inherent in validating the learning gained from experiences, which may have hitherto been denied or ignored, and counting this towards educational or vocational enhancement. But, once again, it is the way in which experiences 'count towards' that causes my disquiet.

Leaving aside the fundamental paradox in MEC/APEL that I discussed above, and its double-edged promise, it is nonetheless true that APEL includes experiential or informal learning, APL increasingly does not. The latter is largely restricted to prior certificated or vocational learning because its value is more often counted in its relevance to the currency of the market place. Much government funding has been spent in developing APL as a means towards acquiring NVQs – a process which is intended to increase vocational competence. Inevitably, APEL's broad-based claim that diverse forms of experience can constitute sources of learning is being muted by the clamour for particular and 'relevant' knowledge which will match the units of 'competence' delineated by the industrial 'lead bodies' who set the NVQ agenda. (Although some claim that such reductionism will be tempered by the broader requirements of the more recent General National Vocational Qualifications – GNVQs.) In other words, the translation of competences from one arena to another is restricted to prior experiences which have a direct bearing upon the nature of the work being assessed. Indeed, the inclusion of prior learning from any source is under threat as NVQ assessors demand evidence of competence in the work currently being undertaken. There are two reasons for this. The assessment of prior learning, if it is to be fair and comprehensive, is a time-consuming and therefore expensive process, particularly if it is conducted at an individual, rather than a group level. The other problem concerns the nature of 'translation'. How much easier it is to assess an employee on the basis of her current work and practices than become involved in the much more complicated task of matching past practice to current relevance – particularly as past practices become obsolete within shorter and shorter spaces of time.

Of course, APL is not used solely in pursuit of vocational enhancement. Many of the new universities – the former polytechnics – (and a growing number of old) incorporate APEL/APL within their admissions procedures, whether to grant access or advanced standing. The theory, once again, is that learning can be acquired from a range of experiences. Once articulated, in the form of general or (even) generic competences, the parity between the skills involved in, for example, running a voluntary self-help group and the traditional entrance requirements for a degree in social work may be self-evident. The reality is that higher education institutions differ in the degree to which such parities are accepted. Academia also delineates its own codes and prescriptions against which an individual's informal learning may all too often be deemed irrelevant and inappropriate. Thence it limits the range of 'accept-able' prior learning to that which falls within, and may be measured against, those codes and prescriptions. The failure of certain Access consortia to include broad-based provision within their terms of reference led in some measure to the insti-tutionalisation (or 'A-levelisation') of Access provision whilst simultaneously excluding areas of experience 'which do not meet the required standard'. (However, recent changes within further education funding mechanisms are encouraging a broader perspective and alliances or partnerships between OCNs and traditional Access consortia.)

Indeed, higher education is currently beset by so many changes that it would be precipitate to form any conclusions as to AP(E)L's future value and function in that sector. As we shall see in Chapter 9, the sea-change affecting institutionalised are-nas of learning such as higher education might render many of our concerns redundant as these traditional sites of education dissemination also become colonised by the philosophy of the market place.

It would therefore be simplistic and misleading of me to appear to be positing an easy dichotomy between APEL as good practice – liberating potential in an open-ended and self-enhancing way; and APL as bad practice – sacrificing process and empowerment at the altar of an outcome-oriented market religion. I would hold to a distinction between the two for the reasons I have outlined but I would hesitate to place relative values on either in terms of what they promise the student.

Of course, dichotomies can be intellectually and politically seductive. In the midst of uncertainty, how much easier it is to adopt an 'either/or' approach and survey the field from the vantage point of the moral high ground. This is a position well known to the WEA – and in many cases for very good reasons. However, many of us who work for the organisation are all too well aware of the compromises, both political and personal, that we have had to face in our continuing struggles to keep its ethos alive.

Making Experience Count and the WEA

The purpose of an adult education worthy of the name is not merely to impart reliable information, important though that is. It is still more to foster the intellectual vitality to master and use it, so that knowledge becomes, not a burden to be borne or a possession to be prized, but a stimulus to constructive thought and an inspiration to action.

R.H. Tawney's words, delivered on the occasion of the fiftieth anniversary of the WEA in 1953, serve as a salutary reminder of how the movement regarded its mission within the broader definitions of adult education. Knowledge does not reside in a vacuum. Its acquisition leads to personal empowerment and political change. And the Statement of Policy appended to the Constitution of 1953 urged the value of adult education:

> *not only as a means of developing individual character and capacity, but as a preparation for the exercise of social rights and responsibilities.*

In 1991, our District, in common with most other WEA regions, was struggling to retain elements of what was conceived by many as an increasingly unfashionable form of provision in the face of financial cuts, constraints and political dictats.

Our liberal programme was threatened with competition from other providers, and the political and financial climate was affecting which courses would flourish and which were no longer 'valid'. Some practitioners were arguing that our liberal provision had become the sole preserve of the relatively privileged; and that we were perilously close to falling on the wrong side of the government's distiction between what it termed 'leisure' education and its definition of 'really useful knowledge'. Our District had always prided itself on maintaining its commitment to work which the Russell Report in 1973 had categorised as special provision. The Report had stressed the need to provide educational opportunity for those within the community who might loosely be termed 'the disadvantaged'. Funding constraints had severely limited the practical implementation of these commitments and we needed to generate money to enable this work to continue. The challenge was how to stake our claim in the educational Brave New World by proving our cost-efficiency and 'relevance' whilst retaining our traditional ethos. Our work in developing experiential learning appeared to provide one opportunity to meet that challenge.

We had run Making Experience Count courses before but various factors had always militated against anything other than a somewhat *ad hoc* approach; and we had learned what the pitfalls were.

There were three key factors which we would have to overcome if we were to mount a programme of courses that would be of value to our students: problems of marginalisation; of standing outwith any formal accrediting structure; and of 'relevance'. I have touched on the issues of the WEA's increasing marginalisation and the 'relevance' of its provision in the world of adult education. A word needs to be said concerning accreditation.

As I have already stated, the subject matter of the MEC/APEL process is the student herself. The 'outcome' could remain at the level of the personal and be measured solely in terms of the student's increased self-esteem. But the outcome might be a portfolio proffered for external validation, assessment and accreditation, and set against educational or vocational enhancement. I also stated that there was a distinction between APEL and APL, with the latter more frequently being linked to vocational outcomes. If external assessment was the outcome sought, then the providers of the AP(E)L programmes had also to be linked to relevant certificating bodies.

The WEA South Eastern District was excluded from any formal accrediting framework within which to offer progression to our students. Whereas we had long prided ourselves on offering broad-based access opportunities (many of our students had gained places in HE as a result of the new-found confidence and learning acquired on our courses) we were excluded from the local Access Consortium as a provider because we did not conform to the stringencies demanded for na-

tional recognition of our provision. We did not provide vocational courses and so could not include APL as a means to gaining units of competence towards an NVQ. There was at the
time no local Open College Network to which we might sue for
recognition. It was deemed impractical at that stage, both financially and logistically, to tap into the London Open College
Federation (LOCF) for the sake of a programme which was to
be run outwith the London area.

And so we return to the difference between public accredi-
bility and private assessment. Given the lack of formal frameworks in which to place our students, we were perilously close
to delivering false promises were we not to stress the sense of
empowerment to be gained from a personal voyage of discovery. The Making Experience Count model would theoretically
enable us to widen our intent and concentrate on the liberatory
aspects that self-acceptance of one's experiential learning could
bring.

If this sounds like a glossy justification for what was actually a decision dictated by expediency then let me urge the sincerity of our commitment. We were convinced of the value of
providing courses which offered a space for student reflection.
We believed that in an increasingly reductionist educational
framework it was vital to fight to retain a commitment to process; we argued that the 'E' in APEL spoke for 'Empowerment'
and its absence in government funded APL/NVQ schemes
spoke for itself.

But we were also aware that the public were looking to accredited outcomes to their courses. If we were to address the
tensions underlying these different perspectives we had to form
links with other organisations and providers. This would enable us to:

- make our provision less marginal
- increase our profile and influence in the field
- work towards informal progression routes
- generate financial support for our courses in the future.

To these ends we worked hard to initiate a network of com-
munications involving a diverse range of statutory and volun-

tary organisations. We made a virtue of, and exploited, the few advantages that our peripheral status conferred. The WEA has a long history of flexibility and collaboration with others. It enjoys a relative freedom from the paradoxical restrictions that power so often confers – other institutions may be the recipients of large-scale public funding, but where money is proffered limitations so often abound.

It has also been generally easier for the WEA to form links because its relative modesty, in organisational terms, makes it freer of the weight of institutional considerations and it can therefore claim the space between others' agendas. Our project was conceived in precisely these terms. With seed-corn funding from the national WEA we used our networks to provide a small-scale yet diverse programme incorporating many levels of educational provision within the single project.

We also initiated the Kent APEL Consortium, which enjoyed representation from the county council, the University of Kent, the careers and guidance service, the Open University, further education, the county adult education service and, of course, the WEA. The story of this network is told in Chapter 10.

The Courses

The project comprised:

- a programme for the unwaged, both women and men, run in conjunction with a local adult education centre
- a programme for women, the majority unwaged, run in conjunction with Brighton Women's Education Branch of the WEA
- a course for women who were known to social services, run in conjunction with the latter
- a course for women and men with acute learning difficulties, run in conjunction with local mental health organisations and voluntary contacts
- a course for women and men in management positions within the Ford Motor Company, run in conjunction

with, and funded by, the Ford Employee Development and Assistance Programme (EDAP)
- a pilot project for women and men who wished to use APEL as a 'fast-route' access course to the part-time degree and diploma programmes at the University of Kent (UKC). This was part of a national pilot which was supported by The Learning From Experience Trust and the Department of Employment.

A word needs to be said in explanation here. I have already mentioned that our work had been excluded from mainstream Access provision as recognised by our local Access consortium. This pilot project at UKC is included here for two important reasons although it was not funded initially by the WEA. I had overall responsibility for the WEA project. I regarded my invitation to teach the UKC pilot as part-recognition of my work with MEC in previous years and I came with a WEA perspective. If the university was going to explore APEL's potential as an alternative form of access then it seemed highly desirable, for the reasons described above, that the facilitation of the course should be undertaken by ourselves.

Thus the story of our project, its diversity of target groups and the nature of our collaborative approaches provides the background to this book. But what began as a typical WEA initiative, outwardly modest yet educationally ambitious and innovative, soon revealed the deepest complexities within the whole MEC/APEL endeavour; and we were forced to question the very principles upon which MEC/APEL's supposed potential for empowerment were predicated.

The course team worked within the WEA's traditional commitment to education for life enhancement, not purely vocational advancement, and, for some at least, within a broader radical tradition of education for social change.

The Structure of the Book

The book is divided into three sections. The first analyses the issues which have arisen in our facilitation of Making Experience

Count within the South Eastern District of the WEA. Chapter 1 discusses some of the key theoretical elements that underpin work in the field of experiential learning and analyses the contribution of the andragogic approach to adult learning. Chapter 2 offers an alternative model – which I have termed gynagogy – and seeks to broaden the debate to incorporate some of the contradictions which andragogy fails to address. Chapter 3 represents a personal account of the learning process. This has been included because analyses of adult learning often read as if there were some distinction between the students on our courses and practitioners in the field. We are all experiential learners, and are equally subject to the complexities that the learning process entails. If I had not included my own experiences, I would have fallen into the trap of objectifying others' stories and making them available for the distanced scrutiny of the detached reader.

The second section describes the courses which were run as the pilot project funded by the national WEA. Chapter 4 describes the recruitment and training of the tutors and acknowledges the exploratory nature of my approach as tutor-trainer. Chapter 5 describes our Making Experience Count course at Ford Motor Company and examines the issues that arise when facilitating personal reflection within a hierarchical and public arena. Chapter 6 is an account of two courses which were designated as 'Outreach' programmes. The first tells the story of our work with a group of women who were approached via local social services. The second is specifically concerned with the needs of a group of adults with learning difficulties and acknowledges the problems inherent in transferring a set of educational assumptions and materials from one student group to another. Chapter 7 discusses the specific issues that arise when facilitating MEC within a single-sex framework. It illustrates the arguments introduced in Chapter 2 and revisits some of the similar concerns described in the first part of Chapter 6. Chapter 8 examines our work with a group of long-term unwaged and highlights the problems that lack of self-esteem brings to the learning process. Chapter 9 concludes this section with an assessment of the value of APEL as an admissions tool for entrance to higher education by concentrating upon the issues that arise when attempting to transpose the learning skills gained in one arena in order to meet the requirements of another.

The third section begins with the story of the Kent APEL Consortium, charts the reasons for its inception and notes its untimely demise. Chapters 11 and 12 describe two recent MEC courses which fall outwith the initial pilot but are set against the background of changes and developments within our provision in the WEA South Eastern District. Chapter 11 discusses the problems inherent in accrediting MEC. Chapter 12 describes our work within a particular ethnic minority community and introduces the question of the cultural transferability of the MEC process.

This book is not the definitive statement upon the process of Making Experience Count. Much has been left out; the rest has been selected and packaged, as in any social encounter of potential advantage, with an eye to approval and acceptance.

Our experiences were messy, contradictory, assured then inconclusive. And to do them justice I retain those contradictions; I veer between personal or individual, and collective or social, concerns. The tone in this volume is at times academic, sometimes acutely personal. The aspects of the lives that we include are not finished, tidy and complete and the issues that arise provoke more questions than answers. This book describes a journey without a destination. The reader, as fellow traveller, will speculate on the far flung horizons according to her own lights and experiences.

SECTION ONE

The Issues

Who what am I? My answer: I am the sum total of everything that went before me, of all I have been seen done, of everything done-to-me. I am everyone everything whose being-in-the-world affected was affected by mine. I am anything that happens after I've gone which would not have happened if I had not come. Nor am I particularly exceptional in this matter; each 'I', every one of the now-six-hundred-million-plus of us, contains a similar multitude. I repeat for the last time: to understand me, you'll have to swallow a world.

Midnight's Children, *Salman Rushdie, 1981, Jonathan Cape.*

CHAPTER ONE

Adults Are What They Have Done

To construct a model – as Palomar was aware – you have to start with something; that is, you have to have principles, from which by deduction, you achieve your own line of reasoning. These principles, also known as postulates, are not something you select, you have them already, because if you did not have them, you could not even begin thinking ('The Model of Models', *from* Mr Palomar, *Italo Calvino, 1983).*

The crucial question for theorists and practitioners of adult learning alike is how experience actually impacts upon the learner so that the knowledge gained can be retained and utilised in different contexts and in the future.

This chapter begins with a brief synopsis of the background to experiential learning and describes the work of two educationalists who have had considerable influence on the theorisation and implementation of MEC/APEL. I then discuss the problems that their approaches entail in terms of the three basic questions that the MEC/APEL process begs:

- the concept of a unified subject enjoying equality of opportunity
- the concept of 'experience' as coherent, consistent and a site for rational intellectual excavation
- parity between the learning gained in one arena and the skills and competences demanded by another.

In order to provide a theoretical underpinning to the discussion, I shall utilise the work of three thinkers who have had significant influence upon the development of philosophical, linguistic and psychoanalytical responses to the paradoxes inherent in trying to understand our selves in relation to the experiences which both form and inform us.

This chapter serves as introduction to issues and questions which will be explored in greater depth as the book proceeds.

The Growth of Experiential Learning as a Movement

The term 'experiential learning' is purely pragmatic, and, as the Concise Oxford Dictionary reminds us, merely refers to the practice of *treating all knowledge as based on experience*. This empirical approach to learning is at the heart of our Western epistemology and can be traced back to Aristotle.

It is the work of John Dewey which is generally accepted as being of seminal influence in the development of experiential learning theory as a challenge to mainstream pedagogic practice. His commitment to the democracy of the classroom, to the relegation of external factors and expectations in favour of internal growth and process are by-words of adult education traditions in general and experiential learning in particular. His understanding and espousal of the fundamentally social nature of learning is a key factor in the work of many later theorists and practitioners who argue that communicative interaction is the basis for learning and change.

Equally important is Dewey's articulation of learning as the recognition of the continuity of experience, with the process of reflection providing the necessary cement between the building blocks of discrete experiences. Reflection is the key to both linking the disparate elements of our experiences into a coherent whole and to facilitating the further connection to our own subjective sense of that cohesion. How else is learning acquired, if not by our selves making subjective sense of the links experience provides?

With the rise of humanistic psychology in the sixties and seventies, experiential learning became part of a wider educational shift which attempted to place the learner at the heart of their own learning process. The terrain was vast; and such was the proliferation of courses, conferences and academic materials purporting to offer alternatives to mainstream pedagogy that experiential learning began to acquire the status of a movement – and one replete with its own orthodoxies and evangelical fervour, despite the diversity of practice the term now incorporated.

In an attempt to understand the way that some of these diverse practices interact (and indeed diverge), it might be helpful to borrow Warner Weil and McGill's (1989) metaphor of the 'four villages' within experiential learning as a way of distinguishing different approaches. The first village is concerned with accrediting learning derived from experience for purposes of entry to educational progression or employment. The second is perceived as utilising experiential learning as a challenge to post-school structures and curricula. The third focuses on social change and the fourth on individual development. We are, therefore, once again faced with the tension between the public and the private outcomes of the experiential learning process. APEL is usually associated with village one because the assessment element was originally conceived as a means of enabling academic entry or enhancing academic potential (Evans, 1988; Warner Weill and McGill, 1989). On this basis, it is perhaps advisable to make a distinction between APEL and MEC because the latter is perceived as an opportunity for reflecting on the learning gained from experience without necessarily proffering the outcomes for external recognition. The problem in making this distinction lies in the central issue of what it means to 'make experience count'. How can we accommodate the potential for individual development without acknowledging the public effects of our learning processes? To what extent can experiential learning be used as a means of effecting social change? Warner Weill and McGill did not perceive the villages as mutually exclusive. Dialogue is meant to ensue between the villages so that 'we are enabled to consider what we intend, and what we do, from new perspectives. Contradictions can become clearer'.

This book describes our experiences in facilitating MEC/APEL across the village boundaries and illustrates the problems that arose when seeking to facilitate individual empowerment whilst not losing sight of broader social issues.

The Influence of Kolb and Knowles

The adult educationalists David Kolb and Malcolm Knowles were key figures in the development of 'orthodox' experiential learning, particularly APEL in its relation to the concerns of village one. Although they have latterly undergone criticism and revision, their arguments were, at one time, central to both the theoretical and the practical dissemination of experiential learning; and their work still informs the basis of Making Experience Count programmes in terms of both ethos and practice – including our own WEA project. Therefore, it is important to be aware of their work and to acknowledge the effect it still has on our thinking. What follows is a brief summary of their key theoretical principles. The issues that their work highlights are then discussed in the rest of this chapter.

Kolb's Learning Cycle is familiar to many educational practitioners. A simple form of it is reproduced below (source Buckle, 1988):

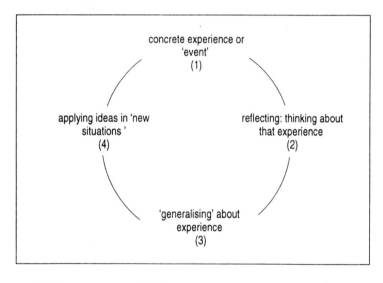

Kolb's argument (Kolb and Fry, 1975; see also Kolb, 1984) stated that:

> *learning and change result from the integration of concrete emotional experiences with cognitive processes: conceptual analysis and understanding.*

In other words, we experience, we reflect, we generalise and then we act. But, as Dewey reminds us, experience does not occur in a vacuum, and therefore it would be useful to examine the background to Kolb's conclusions.

In 1946, a group of colleagues – Lewin, Lippitt, Bradford and Benne – had been asked by the Connecticut State Interracial Commission to design a new approach to leadership and group dynamics training. They had begun the programme by encouraging an interactive and egalitarian relationship between the staff and the participants. At the end of the first day, the research staff collated the experiences of the day in preparation for the next. It was judged best to exclude the participants from this assessment for fear of causing harm. However, a small group asked to join them and Lippitt recorded the result. It is worth quoting at length (Kolb and Fry, 1975):

> Sometime during the evening, an observer made some remarks about the behaviour of one of the three persons who were sitting in – a woman trainee. She broke in to disagree with the observation and described it from her point of view. For a while there was quite an active dialogue between the research observer, the trainer and the trainee about the interpretation of the event, with Kurt (Lewin) an active prober, obviously enjoying this different source of data that had to be coped with and integrated ... The evening session from then on became the significant learning experience of the day, with the focus on actual behavioural events and with active dialogue about differences of interpretation and observations of the events by those who had participated in them.

Thus the scene had been set and the events recorded. What is fascinating is the nature of the conceptual leap that Kolb made from these observations. He gave centrality to the role that tension and conflict must play for learning to take place, 'learning is by its very nature a tension- and conflict-filled process', and concluded that 'New knowledge, skills or attitudes are achieved through confrontation among the four perspectives in the experiential learning model.' These perspectives, or abilities, he labelled 'concrete experience (CE), reflective observation (RO), abstract conceptualisation (AC) (and) active experimentation (AE)'; and stated that, if the learner were to be effective he (sic) needed to be able to utilise all four abilities. Acknowledging that this was somewhat idealistic, he formulated the Learning Style Inventory (LSI) which categorised types of learners within the four stages, matched these types to further categorisations of career or profession, and was able to conclude that: 'people choose fields which are consistent with their learning styles and are further shaped to fit the learning norms of their field once they are in it.'

His conclusions may be summarised as follows:

- learning is a cyclical process and represents the integration between concrete experience and cognitive assessment
- there are four stages to this process which give rise to four types of learner, because few of us can utilise all of the stages equally
- we seek the kinds of employment which are consistent with our learning styles.

We may derive from these conclusions that, in order to improve the learning abilities of our students, we should encourage practice in the learning styles with which they are less familiar. In other words, awareness of the whole learning cycle can only encourage greater understanding and improve potential. Yet Kolb takes the process one step further by emphasising the element of tension noted earlier. Whilst allowing for a dialectical relationship between experience and assessment, consistent with the cyclical approach, he posits a developmental model which seems to suggest that if learning is to be derived from experience, then the latter must be conflict-ridden: 'growth proceeds from a state of embededness, defensiveness, dependency and reaction to a state of self-actualization, independence, pro-action and self-direction.'

These conclusions echo those of Malcolm Knowles (1980). It is he who is commonly attributed with the popularisation of the term 'andragogy', although he first heard the word used by an educator from former Yugoslavia.

Andragogy is meant to encompass the accumulated learning from disciplines as diverse as 'clinical psychology, developmental   psychology   ...   gerontology,   sociology   and anthropology', which educators have combined with their experience as teachers to posit a 'comprehensive, coherent theory of adult learning'. The practice is distinguished from pedagogy, which literally means the leading (or teaching) of children, because andragogy 'is based on the Greek word aner (with the stem *andr-*) meaning "man", not boy, or "adult". '

And we are reminded of Kolb in Knowles' psychological definition of adulthood. It is the point at which individuals perceive themselves to be essentially self-directing:

> *So if you ask adults who they are they are likely to identify themselves by describing what their occupations are, where they have worked, where they have travelled, what their training and experience have equipped them to do, and what their achievements have been. Adults are what they have done (Knowles, 1980: 50).*

Knowles' theoretical model was largely based upon a combination of Maslow's famous 'hierarchy of human needs' and Erik Erikson's 'eight ages of man', which elucidates the stages we must travel towards maturation. The following is his synthesis of the two (from Knowles, 1980):

DIMENSIONS OF MATURATION

From:	*Toward:*
1. Dependence	Autonomy
2. Passivity	Activity
3. Subjectivity	Objectivity
4. Ignorance	Enlightenment
5. Small abilities	Large abilities
6. Few responsibilities	Many responsibilities
7. Narrow interests	Broad interests
8. Selfishness	Altruism
9. Self-rejection	Self-acceptance
10. Amorphous self-identity	Integrated self-identity
11. Focus on particulars	Focus on principles
12. Superficial concerns	Deep concerns
13. Imitation	Originality
14. Need for certainty	Tolerance for ambiguity
15. Impulsiveness	Rationality

I offer a critique of this approach and Knowles' model in Chapter 2. For our current purposes we need only note that in the work of both Kolb and Knowles, and in the assumptions underlying the development of APEL as part of the experiential 'movement', we see a consistency in terms of the three basic precepts outlined in the Introduction:

- the concept of a unified subject enjoying equality of opportunity
- the concept of 'experience' as coherent, consistent and a site for rational intellectual excavation

and, less obvious but still implicit:

- parity between the learning gained in one arena and the skills and competences demanded by another.

Thus the role of the educator is to facilitate the satisfaction of individual need and the achievement of individual goals by encouraging the learner in their journey towards fullest expression of their potential.

I now discuss each of these assumptions in turn by drawing upon a number of counter-perspectives which engage with the issues in different ways, but which share a profound unease with the proposition that 'adults are what they have done'.

The Concept of a Unified Subject

A model is by definition that in which nothing has to be changed, that which works perfectly; whereas reality, as we see clearly, does not work and constantly falls to pieces; so we must force it, more or less roughly, to assume the form of the model (Mr Palomar, *Italo Calvino, 1983*).

Dewey's (1963) view of learning as an 'experiential continuum' was dependent upon an interactive process between tutor and student, with the former acknowledging the effects of social, environmental and prior experiences upon the receptivity of the latter:

> *The basic characteristic of habit is that every experience enacted and undergone modifies the one who acts and undergoes, while this modification affects, whether we wish it or not, the quality of subsequent experiences.*

The developmental or cyclical models of learning discussed above may be consistent with Dewey up to this point, but they neither acknowledge nor explain the full impact of the sentence which follows: *'For it is a somewhat different person who enters into them'*.

What did Dewey mean by this? Was he articulating that experience, which I can only assume to be common, wherein we feel that different social circumstances bring forth different 'selves' in us? How many of us have looked back to the past and declared, 'I was a different person then'? Yet, at the same time, how many of us have acknowledged the 'changes' only to reiterate that 'the real me hasn't changed at all, of course'?

If we are to understand the complexity inherent in the notion of experiential learning, we have to address the relationship between our 'selves' and the society with which we engage. Such a pursuit requires an understanding of some of the theoretical positions which have attempted to unravel that relationship. What follows is a personal interpretation of some of those debates. Each is clothed in its own jargon, and I am aware that the more I write, the more I move away from a sense of the totality of what I am trying to express. This is not an anti-intellectual stance. This is merely a plea for patience as I try and match the beat of the theoretical to the rhythm of the practitioner in the field. (It is interesting to note in passing that this ordering of events, with the sudden leap to the realm of generalisation is precisely the reverse of Kolb's process in the learning cycle. If what follows is not rooted in experience and followed by reflection before conclusions are reached, then learning has not taken place.)

One of the cornerstones of the Western epistemological tradition has been the relationship between the 'knower' and the 'known'; between the individual and the 'outside world'; between the subject and society. It has been epitomised in the Cartesian dictum *'cogito ergo sum'*, which marked the Age of Reason and assured the pre-eminence of the subject 'I' as unified and coherent. Knowledge represented the rational mind's acquisition of facts about the objective world.

This robust expression of individuality went hand-in-glove with positivism (the objectivity of science) and empiricism (the objectivity of rational thinking). It was associated, in turn, with classic liberalism; the political attempt to protect the rights of the 'free man' (sic) from undue let or hindrance in order that he may fulfil his individual potential (as long as his pursuit did not limit that of another).

God was not dead ... yet. But, as Henriques *et al.* point out (1984) an all-embracing humanism (tended) 'to see the individual as the agent of all social phenomena and production including knowledge'.

Marx attacked the bourgeois complacency of the notion of the 'free individual', but his economic determinism, whilst challenging the supremacy of the Cartesian subject, substituted for the latter an equally powerful and monolithic structure based on class rather than individual interest. Of course, there have been a number of thinkers who have tempered the reductionism of functionalist Marxism but none has adequately accounted for the complexity of the interactive individual/societal relationship.

There had been other attacks on the notion of the unified subject which we must not overlook. Freud had compounded the problem of the coherent 'I' by reminding us of the power of the unconscious, of the irrational elements in our make-up which have always mocked the power of reason and challenged rationality with the dark play of hidden desires.

Feminism has also criticised the patriarchal assumptions inherent in the Cartesian subject; where does the supremacy of 'rational man' leave the wants and needs of women?

One influential approach to dealing with this issue has argued the need to deconstruct the assumption of a unified, or coherent, subject. It is suggested that only then can we hope to understand individual/societal interaction and answer the dilemma posed by Dewey and explain the somewhat different person who enters into subsequent experiences. Deconstruction:

> *involves prising apart the meanings and assumptions fused together in the ways we understand ourselves in order to see*

them as historically specific products rather than timeless and incontrovertible given facts. Such an analysis of the construction of the modern form of individuality is a prerequisite for understanding and bringing about change.

(For this quotation and for the explanations which follow, I am indebted to the work of Henriques *et al.* (1984), who have provided us with a straightforward and comprehensive account of human 'agency' in their book *Changing the Subject: Psychology, social regulation and subjectivity*.)

And it is feminism that we must thank for this dramatic intellectual shift. It has consistently urged the need for a politics of transformation based upon a sophisticated analysis of the deconstructed subject in the face of the intellectual inadequacy of the notion of a coherent 'I'. Feminism:

has introduced into the politics of change the necessity of understanding consciousness as something produced rather than as the source of ideas and the social world — as constituted and not constitutive (Henriques et al., *1984).*

In other words, we do not pre-date our social relations, we are formed in relation to them; we are constituted as part of the complex web which comprises what we term 'society'. But we are not merely composite parts of some relentless engine of control; neither do we enjoy complete free will and ring-side seats at some spectacle called 'reality' upon which we lay judgement.

But the crucial questions still remain unanswered. How are we socialised into the mores of the culture in which we find ourselves? How are we positioned as protagonists on the stage of our particular set of gendered, economic and cultural circumstances? What does it mean to state that *'we do not pre-date our social relations'*, and how do we account for that illusory sense of self which both knows its past, yet marvels at our present distance from it? I shall look at the work of three theorists, from the disciplines of philosophy, linguistics and psychoanalysis, who have attempted their own answers to these problems.

The work of Michel Foucault provides further impetus to our endeavours because he problematises not only the concept of the 'individual' but of 'society' as well. His 'discourse theory' was founded on the belief that specific historical circumstances generate interest in, and intervention in, social practice. Henriques *et al.* have furnished us with the following example of this, which illustrates quite clearly the confusion that arises when hitherto 'taken for granted' methods of socialisation are disrupted by other influences; and 'natural' developmental processes are shown to be predicated upon a mix of contingent social, biological, political and economic factors.

The staple diet of a large number of Americanised Puerto Ricans was chickens; chickens fed on animal feed containing oestrogen. The diet had catastrophic effects on the sexual maturation of young girls, with some showing full breast development and menstruating at four years. The result for the community was utter bewilderment at not knowing how to behave appropriately towards these women/girls. The mainly American corporations controlling the local agribusiness resisted calls to change the formula for the chicken feed. The problem was therefore biological, social, political and economic.

To return to Foucault, this example illustrates that there are a number of 'discourses' generating their own dynamics and yet enmeshing within the 'discursive complex' that constitutes any given situation. All discourses are regulated and systematic, and are further ruled by their interplay with, and difference from, other discourses. Thence the role of 'deconstruction' mentioned above. In order to understand how discourses operate as they do, deconstruction is necessary because it 'retraces the system of "dependencies" of a discourse'.

Thus we can see that Foucault's contribution to our debate is his deconstruction of the unifying assumption behind the word 'society'. If we replace the term with the much more flexible concept of the 'social', we can view it more clearly as the site of an ever-changing interplay of various discursive dynamics and relations of power. The complex interplay of factors affecting the Puerto Rican situation could only be understood by deconstructing them and tracing their roots to the biological, social, political and economic, as mentioned above.

What Foucault helps us to realise is that there are a number of areas which combine to create the complexity of social situations and interactions. It would therefore be insufficient, from educational (and political) perspectives, to adopt a singular approach to the problem by assuming a coherent model of 'experience' with which to deal with the problems within the Puerto Rican community. In other words, if we were to organise an education project for the community in the form of a Making Experience Count programme, it would be sheer folly to seek to empower our 'students' by starting from the assumption that they 'are what they have done'. Their confusions about what they were doing stemmed from a much more fundamental crisis around the nexus of factors which had challenged the basis of who they were. Making Experience Count, if it were to help this community, would have to begin by unravelling the nexus and then encourage a collective response based upon a shared understanding of a common problem.

This is familiar territory to those engaged in community education, or education for social change. Indeed, the tensions surrounding educational responsibility, in terms of facilitating individual or collective empowerment, are a key feature of this book and will be explored in greater detail in later chapters.

But for our present purposes, I shall return to Foucault. As we have seen, his contribution to our understanding of the complexity inherent in social engagement was in urging the deconstruction of the several 'discourses', the economic, biological and so on, that comprise that complexity. However, Foucault would argue that none of the discourses is privileged as the root cause of all the others; it is their *mutual dependencies* which generate the sense of power that is overwhelming the Puerto Rican community. I have a problem with this. Whilst agreeing that mutual dependencies do exist among regulatory practices, I would be forgiven for assuming that certain discourses appropriate more power than others and thence set the others in motion. The problem would not have arisen for the Puerto Rican community were it not for the presence of the American business concern.

The issue of power is a crucial area of muddle in Foucault's argument, but this need not negate his contribution to our debate. His importance lies in the linkage between his deconstruction of 'society' and the concomitant deconstruction of the notion of the 'individual' or 'subject'; and that this is equally acknowledged to be:

the effect of a production, caught in the mutually constitutive
web of social practices, discourses and subjectivity; its reality
is the tissue of social relations (Henriques et al., 1984).

We can now begin to understand the sense of fragmentation we sometimes feel in the face of the several selves we have
to adopt in order to fulfil our social roles; to understand the
Deweyan notion that 'it is a somewhat different person who enters ... subsequent experiences'. But before we examine the implications of these conclusions it is important to appreciate the
part that the theorisation of language has played in these debates. Foucault could not have articulated his 'discourse theory'
were it not for the work of the turn of the century linguist, Fer-
dinand de Saussure.

To put it simply, Saussure's work challenged the traditional
relationship between the word and the object it represented.
Whereas that relationship had generally been perceived as a
one-to-one correspondence – the word 'rose' *meant* the flower in
our garden – Saussure argued that the relationship was contingent upon the 'sign systems' or social practices which, in turn,
delineated meaning according to their relationship to other sign
systems and social practices.

If we take as example the word 'cat' most of us would picture a furry, four-legged creature that chases mice. But if
pressed for further associations, we might offer terms such as
'sleek, 'sensual'; even 'feminine'. To compare these associations
with those of an ancient Egyptian, who worshipped the cat as a
deity, would reveal not only the cultural specificity of language,
but also provide certain clues as to how particular discourses,
for example that of the feminine, reveal societal preoccupations
in their formation.

Foucault extended the argument to illustrate the 'contradictory subjectivity' we experience as a result of the confusions
and irrationalisms we suffer because we are positioned in certain discursive complexes. But he did not explain how we came
to be situated within these lingusitic sign systems, neither could
he answer the paradox of the self – that feeling of fragmentation
underpinned by a sense of continuity.

Henriques *et al.* ask:

> *But how are such fragments held together? Are we to assume*
> *... that the individual subject is simply the sum total of all*
> *positions in discourses since birth? If this is the case, what*
> *accounts for the continuity of the subject, and the subjective*
> *experience of identity? What accounts for the predictability*
> *of people's actions, as they repeatedly position themselves*
> *within particular discourses?*

And they introduce the work of the psychoanalyst Jacques Lacan to provide an explanation.

Lacan has also been appropriated by some feminists seeking to account not only for our experience of identity, but also in order to understand the particular 'societal preoccupations' in the formation of discourses as noted above, and thence, the relative power that certain societal formations so readily wield.

> *(It) is the entry into language which is the precondition for*
> *becoming conscious or aware of oneself as a distinct entity*
> *within the terms set by pre-existing social relations and*
> *cultural laws ... this process simultaneously founds the*
> *unconscious. Since language is by definition a social system*
> *... the social enters into the formation of the unconscious*
> *(Henriques et al., 1984).*

Borrowing from Freud, Lacan also contends that the prime and universal 'signifier' (provider of linguistic meaning) is the phallus, thus explaining the apparently universal experience of women as socially marginalised in relation to men because women are situated in language, and therefore in society, in a relation of 'lack'. They are defined as 'other' to the masculine 'subject'.

Before we throw Lacan out of court completely, it has to be said in his defence that he was being descriptive, not prescriptive; and did not attribute any essentialist characteristics to the 'natures' of men and women.

In other words, it is the power play of different societal discourses (ways of naming) which accords value or otherwise to the positions we occupy in the social arena – which places us in our relative distances from the central loci of control. If we take another example; just as language reflects the subordinate position of women, 'black', in our society, is situated in a relation of 'lack' to 'white'.

At one level, we can be forgiven for saying at this juncture, 'so what?' Lacan might have proffered an account of the subject's relation to societal inequity in terms of the language we use, but he did not move the argument beyond reflections upon the *status quo*. What he did offer, however, was an analysis of the paradox at the heart of our sense of our own subjectivity; that feeling that we are both many selves and yet perhaps one underlying the many. Once again, he borrows from Freud.

Lacan accounts for the paradox by positing an elaboration of the Oedipus Complex called the Mirror Phase. The dyadic unit of mother and child, which produces the child's sense of satisfaction and completion or wholeness, has to be ruptured at the first experience of absence from the mother. The child's own mirror reflection will never compensate for the totality of the 'reflection' given by the mother.

> *In Lacan's account, the child uses his or her first words to establish, in fantasy, control over the loss of the object which gave satisfaction. As words displace the original object, we see the first step in the process of repression which forms the unconscious; entry into language inaugurates the production of subjectivity (Henriques et al., 1984).*

This subjectivity is gendered according to the prime signifier, and in relation to the interplay of other discursive practices which hold cultural and societal sway. It is also predicated upon that initial sensation of loss. Hence the paradox:

> *though we may have a sense of our own identity and feel that we are the source from which our thoughts emanate, these experiences are far from constant and cannot necessarily be captured at will; we continually struggle to find a continuity to our being ... the 'I' of the cogito ... is illusory and forever unattainable (Henriques et al., 1984).*

Our sense of continuity in our own subjectivity derives from our repeated, and always futile, attempts to close the gap on our initial loss.

As 'Mr Palomar' reminded us at the beginning of this section, reality does not work and so we must force it to assume the form of a model. Yet, however inadequate the models of Foucault or Lacan might be, they have articulated the paradox at the heart of our sense of self and challenged the first premise upon which we suggested MEC/APEL was based. The Puerto Rican example has illustrated the nonsense behind the claim for the concept of a unified subject enjoying equality of opportunity.

The Concept of Experience as Coherent, Consistent and a Site for Rational Intellectual Excavation

The preceding argument has already cast doubt upon notions of coherence and consistency. I should now like to explore the problems behind the assumption that experience is also a site for rational intellectual excavation. What I meant by stating this as one of the precepts upon which MEC was based was the assumption implicit in the role that reflection has to play in the learning cycle. Kolb is quite clear that for learning to take place we must progress from the experience, via reflection, to theorisation, thence understanding and application of our new knowledge in another sphere. He acknowledges that the cycle rarely works as smoothly as this and that our learning styles indicate our bias toward one activity over the others. Yet the role of reflection remains crucial in being able to extricate the learning gained from experience. The assumption that the reflective process is rational and cognitive, or intellectual, is also implicit as a first step towards understanding or making sense of experience. Indeed, the cycle itself was the result of the rationalisation of a group experience and the conclusions derived from it.

Kolb also posited a developmental model which we saw was echoed in the work of Malcolm Knowles. They both argued that growth proceeds 'from a state of embededness and dependency to one of independence and self-direction'. Kolb asserted that conflict was the crux, the resolution of which produced the learning.

As we shall see in later chapters, many of the materials which have been produced for the facilitation of MEC are predicated at some level upon this conflictual model of development. I am not suggesting that Kolb was proposing that his idea of conflict should be conflated with the notion that painful experiences provide learning. However, the assumption underlying much work with MEC is that our painful experiences are rich seams to mine in order to extract learning. Whilst we may concur with the view that we learn as much, if not more, from our suffering, the assumption that these painful experiences are suitable materials for the classroom poses a series of crucial questions about the roles and responsibilities of the facilitators. This would not be an issue if the process of reflection were simply one of straightforward intellectual reclamation. The reality for those of us who have facilitated MEC is that such an assumption is false. This will be explored in greater depth in Chapters 2 and 3 and in those which discuss our case studies. For our current purposes, I would like to return to the original learning experience from which Kolb drew his conclusions and suggest a re-reading of the situation (Kolb and Fry, 1975):

> *Sometime during the evening, an observer made some remarks about the behaviour of one of the three persons who were sitting in – a woman trainee. She broke in to disagree with the observation and described it from her point of view. For a while there was quite an active dialogue ... with Kurt an active prober, obviously enjoying this different source of data that had to be coped with and integrated.*

What was the nature of the provocative remarks? Were they sexist? They obviously caused the woman some disquiet. The ensuing dialogue was 'active'. Does that mean healthily egalitarian or typical of repressive exchanges in a male-dominated environment? 'Kurt, an active prober, obviously (enjoyed) this different source of data', and yet the conclusion was that learning is by its very nature a tension- and conflict-filled process. Does that mean that Kurt enjoyed tension and conflict, or that his status as researcher allowed him to observe the woman's unease and record it for posterity? What would her conclusions have been – that conflict is necessary for growth and the process is a dialectical mix between four discrete stages – or that her learning had been inhibited by assumptions about her behaviour, that intervention cost her dear, that the ensuing evening sessions were established to forestall a repetition of misunderstanding, conflict and resentment? Perhaps she would have gained more of lasting value had she enjoyed a secure environment in which to explore tentatively and intuitively her own analysis of the relationship between leaders and groups. She might even have concluded that learning is not a dialectical or developmental process but a synthesis between the felt and the known which is somehow greater than either and yet dependent on both, so that to categorise one would damage the other; to tear them asunder would destroy the whole.

This re-reading is purely speculative, but it is offered as a reminder that adult learning models are usually predicated on the assumption that the masculine norm and the adult norm are one and the same. One of the few challenges to this approach is offered by Belenky *et al.*'s important work *Women's Ways of Knowing. The development of self, voice and mind* (1986). I shall be discussing the implications of their findings in the following chapter, which explores the limitations of theoretical positions which assume that 'adult' and 'man' are synonymous. For the present discussion I would just like to note that their conclusions, after working with 135 women, are highly relevant to our discussion on Kolb:

> *People are said to be precipitated into states of cognitive conflict when, for example, some external event challenges their ideas and the effort to resolve the conflict leads to cognitive growth. We do not deny that cognitive conflict can act as an impetus to growth; all of us can attest to such experiences in our own lives. But in our interviews only a handful of women described a powerful and positive learning experience in which a teacher aggressively challenged their notions ... On the whole, women found the experience of being doubted debilitating rather than energizing (Belenky et al., 1986).*

I am not suggesting, of course, that we should dispense with Kolb altogether: his value lies in his expression within the learning cycle of capacities other than the purely cognitive. Inclusion of the affective, the perceptive and the behavioural argues for an integrated model of learning which is crucial to experientialists. What I am exploring is the efficacy of the models at our disposal when dealing with the realms of experience, because I believe this process to be a much more delicate and complex interaction than is generally either acknowledged or accounted for.

Parity Between the Learning Gained in One Arena and the Skills and Competences Demanded by Another

The problems underlying this assumption will be dealt with more fully in the chapters describing the MEC courses that comprised our project. The preceding discussion has introduced issues concerning social inequity and the complex interrelationship between our sense of self and the experiences which inform that sensibility. Given such complexity, it is highly spurious to posit an easy match between the learning gained in one arena and that required by another – unless one is talking the language of skills and competences, and at the most superficial level. Once again, we seem to be making a distinction between APL and its concern for the transferability of skills, and APEL, which appears to be claiming a much broader base from which to operate.

If we are to make sense of this conundrum, we have to address the differences between skills and competences, learning and education. At its most basic, we have to unpack the notion of generic skills, recognise the social constructions integral to their expression and then pose the question of transferability.

APEL assumes that skills are generic and can be used in a number of different contexts. This is its liberatory promise for advancement in the public realm. But how realistic is this in a society constructed along divisions of class, race and gender? Is the translation of nurturing skills acquired in the home to a job as carer within the social services, for example, sufficient to warrant APEL's claims as a liberatory mechanism for women?

I would suggest that APEL, whilst encouraging the translation of so-called generic competences, is all too often reinforcing the *status quo*. If we attack APL for its narrow reductionism, we have to be wary of the APEL evangelism, which, by fostering the 'uniqueness of the individual', is actually maintaining the ethic of 'difference' and inequity upon which our social constructions are based, and ghettoising distinctions between us so as to inhibit shared understanding which might foster collective change.

This is not to throw APEL out with the APL bath water. The following chapters attest to the potential for change that an MEC course may offer. But they also illustrate the contradictions inherent in our notions of empowerment, and alert us to the dangers that lie in forgetting that the learning process is ultimately a social process which can have profound social implications.

CHAPTER TWO

Gendered Reflections: Notes Towards Gynagogy

Adult learners do not bring their experiences with them into education; they are their experience (Knowles, 1978). But the answers to the real complexities and challenges of this idea do not seem to lie simply in modular programmes, access courses, distance- or open-learning initiatives, experiential learning or andragogy. They lie in much finer nuances of expressing respect, concern and care for individuals, and in giving priority to the need for adults to build upon and make sense of their own and others' 'life worlds' (Wildemeersch, quoted by Warner Weil, 1989).

The preceding chapter took issue with the simplicity of the premise that 'adults are what they have done'. This chapter extends the discussion by concentrating on the nature of women's experiences.

The reasons for this approach are three-fold. Our work with MEC has highlighted the inefficacy of adopting a pedagogic programme based on the assumption that the masculine norm and the adult norm are necessarily one and the same. Our work has always sought to validate the specificity of particular groups' experiences, and encourage hitherto silent voices to be heard as precursors to individual and collective growth and change. But the third point is perhaps the most crucial.

The world has moved on since the blossoming of the second feminist wave in the late 1960s. It is an undeniable fact that many women enjoy increased opportunities in both the public and the private spheres. Many more women hold positions of authority in a greater range of professions. Increased Access opportunities have enabled larger numbers of women to enter higher and further education. Discourses relating to the whole arena of sexual mores have broadened the range of representations available to women in the expression of their 'private' lives and needs.

Twenty-five years ago, the energy generated by the women's movement found expression in easily identifiable causes and complaints. Of course, there were conflicts between women from the outset. Radical feminists viewed the 'universal oppression' of women as a result of generalised patriarchal power and authority. Liberal feminists believed that changes in legislation could 'right the wrongs' of sexual inequity. Socialist feminists argued that the problem was economic and urged solidarity with other victims of capitalist oppression. But the changes wrought in the intervening quarter century have torn the concept of 'sisterhood' asunder and problematised the very notion of 'women' as an homogeneous group with shared experiences, beliefs and values.

The issues surrounding female circumcision provide a case in point. At a conservative estimate 74 million women worldwide suffer some form of genital mutilation (McLean, 1980). Feminists in the Majority World have attacked feminists in the West for gross insensitivity in their broad condemnation of the practice. The former have argued that the problem represents a complex interplay of cultural, political and economic factors, each generating its own dynamics, including the passionate advocacy of many of the women involved. The problem for Western feminists, therefore, is how to sustain the idea of 'global sisterhood' in the face of different cultural imperatives. To adopt a Foucauldian analysis would allow for an understanding of the various discourses involved in the issue; but it would relativise the factors involved and deny any easy reliance on fundamental cause – and therefore blame. To put it simply, in the case of female circumcision the women involved are not uniformly, or only, oppressed by male power and control.

If we return to the Minority World, feminists have pointed out the difficulty in articulating the nature of shared experience between women of different class, colour and sexuality and have argued against the easy sloganising which generalises men as 'the enemy' and then posits solutions in separatism or equal rights (Ramazanoglu, 1989; Gunew, 1990).

Yet as a feminist adult educator, working largely with women, I find little comfort in the greater understanding that relativist analyses such as Foucault's can offer. I know the dangers inherent in claiming that women share fundamental experiences because they are women. Given the complexities outlined above, such a belief can only rest on a narrow adherence to the paramount importance of the 'natural' or 'biological' differences between the sexes. In claiming that 'women are women and men are men' this argument maintains the *status quo* by precluding any possibility of change. But the social constructionist argument, outlined in Chapter 1, which holds that women and men are placed in relative and sometimes contradictory spheres of authority and control, does not account for my *experience* of women being more than the sum of our socially constructed parts. Whilst I might agree intellectually with Rothfield (1990) that it 'is no longer possible to assume a univocal epistemological project for women', I have empathy with the emotional implications of her concluding clause in the following explication:

> *Feminist excursions into the terrain of sexuality and sexual difference have come to ascribe an ensemble of levels to the female subject, such that networks of desire, conscious thought, unconscious repressions, and complexes may be interwoven, producing paradoxes, tensions, and ruptures.*

It is in order to try and heal the 'rupture' between theoretical understanding and practical experience of my own and other women's lives that the rest of this chapter is written. It is important to stress at this stage that what follows is consistent with the tenor of the book as a whole. In the Introduction, I noted that our experiences in facilitating MEC had revealed many of the paradoxes at the heart of our endeavours; and that the elaboration of these would necessarily mirror some of the contradictions involved. I feel that the same must be said about the ensuing feminist analysis. Many women have been alienated by the abstractions and complexities of much feminist theory. I do not wish to debate the rights and wrongs of this. I would rather retrace some of the basic steps by which many of the more abstruse conclusions have been reached and explore the resonance and relationships with the main themes of the book. Therefore I shall organise the material in accordance with the main task in hand, which is to examine the relevance and efficacy of the learning models upon which APEL, and particularly MEC, is based. I begin by proffering a critique of andragogy from a feminist perspective. I then examine some of the work which has been undertaken in relation to women and memory because it highlights issues which are crucial to our understanding of the role of reflection in the MEC process. I then return to the question of the 'nature' of women's experiences in order to assess the extent to which they may, indeed, be counted.

In Place of Andragogy

We thus construct ourselves and our emotions out of the raw materials of our particular experiences which occur at particular historical times and in particular social contexts and places. In so constructing ourselves, we sometimes acquiesce and take on the social meanings, and sometimes we resist and transform these meanings (Crawford et al., 1992).

As I noted when outlining certain andragogic principles in Chapter 1, much has been written in direct refutation of the usefulness of the model (Davenport, 1987). I do not intend to reiterate those arguments here. My concern is to question the validity of andragogy's assumption that the masculine model of development is synonymous with the adult.

Knowles (1980) notes that in order to distinguish between the teaching of children – pedagogy – and the teaching of adults, educators 'coined the label "andragogy" which is based on the Greek word *aner* (with the stem *andr-*) meaning "man, not boy" or "adult" '. Herein lies the problem, and it is double-edged. Feminists have long taken issue with the 'phallocentrism' inherent in assuming the masculine as the universal, e.g.

'manpower', 'mankind', and have argued that just as language creates and reflects our world so such linguistic colonisation of the feminine reflects the power imbalance between the sexes. But even if Knowles acknowledged this and changed the terminology, andragogy is predicated upon an individualistic model of achievement which is largely gender (and class) specific.

In her influential text *Subject Women*, Oakley (1981) includes a table of the 'attributes of good female and male students', i.e. those characteristics receiving teachers' – and society's – approbation. Although the list was compiled in the 1960s, it is worth examining in detail. It is not proffered as *proof* of gender bias within educational structures, but rather as emblematic of deeper societal preoccupations.

Adjectives describing good female students	*Adjectives describing good male students*
Appreciative	Active
Calm	Adventurous
Conscientious	Aggressive
Considerate	Assertive
Co-operative	Curious
Mannerly	Energetic
Poised	Enterprising
Sensitive	Frank
Dependable	Independent
Efficient	Inventive
Mature	
Obliging	
Thorough	

(Source: Kemener, 1965, quoted in Oakley, 1981)

The majority of adjectives describing the 'good female student' are approbations of self *in relation to others*. The same is patently not true for the boys. It is also noteworthy that *being* for a boy is synonymous with *doing* and *acting*; for a girl the synonyms are *caring* and *responding*. And we are reminded that, for Knowles, the definition of adulthood is predicated upon the former (1980):

When people define themselves as adults ... they see themselves increasingly as producers or doers ... They see themselves as being able to make their own decisions and face the consequences, to manage their own lives.

For despite the fact that these lists are almost 30 years old, I believe they remain painfully relevant to many women today; and, in particular, to the majority of women in our classes. For the tragedy of 'woman' in our culture is that she is still given major responsibility for interaction with others. There is nothing intrinsically wrong with the characteristics attributed to her. But as we saw in Chapter 1, subjectivities, and therefore experiences of the world, are constructed in relation to prevailing discourses. As long as society privileges masculine self-actualisation and equates masculine attributes with adulthood it does so at the expense of the positively nurturing and responsible attributes of the 'feminised' woman. Thus, her pre-defined 'caring and sharing' role is at constant variance with her strivings for autonomy; and we have to ask at what psychic cost is she likely to fulfil Knowles' definition of adulthood as the 'point at which individuals perceive themselves to be essentially self-directing'?

Perhaps a clue lies in Sheehy's (1974) analysis of adult development, undertaken as a longitudinal study and completed in 1969. If we regard Knowles' model as a reflection of societal imbalance in the way our gendered paths to adulthood are constructed then we need not be surprised by Sheehy's conclusions:

Men became more dependable, productive and assertive ... At the same time, their control was achieved with the loss of some tenderness and self-expressiveness. [Whereas women had become] ... submissive, fearful, guilty, over-controlled and hostile. Their only developmental gains were those associated with being a wife and mother. They were more protective, introspective, and sympathetic ... but their only security was in the role of mother.

In this context, it is interesting to compare the lists of gendered characteristics outlined above with Knowles' 'dimensions of maturation' model discussed in the preceding chapter. His contention was that we should all strive to move from the 'dependency' model on the left of the equation towards the 'autonomous' model on the right. On the basis of our current discussion, I would argue that women have a harder road to travel.

I am acutely aware that at the start of this chapter I argued that the world had changed significantly during the past 25 years, and that many more opportunities had become available to women. But what has not altered is the fact that women are still held to be fundamentally responsible for meeting and servicing society's affective needs. Thus, the relative plethora of opportunities which may be available in the public sphere still have to be negotiated in relation to the private – *and with a range of psychic consequences reminiscent of those described by Sheehy two decades ago.* This is not to say that the differences between women in terms of colour and class are eradicated by the similarities of their responsibilities in the private sphere. This would be patently ridiculous. Some women have the financial power to alleviate some of the burdens of domestic responsibility. (And in our climate of economic insecurity, many men find themselves restricted to, or even choosing, the domestic realm.) However, women's subjectivities – their sense of themselves – remain generally situated, in societal terms, in relation to the needs of others. This fact has profound consequences within a learning environment seeking to 'make sense of women's experiences'. If we accept the fact that men are much more likely to see themselves as potentially 'self-directing' than women, then it is highly likely that the sexes will demand different approaches and articulate different needs.

> *The elusive mystery of women's development lies in its recognition of the continuing importance of attachment in the human life cycle. Woman's place in man's life cycle is to protect this recognition while the developmental litany intones the celebration of separation, autonomy,*

individuation, and natural rights (Gilligan, 1979; quoted by Tennant, 1988).

This is why I have subtitled this chapter 'notes towards gynagogy'. I am not seeking to replace the gender bias inherent in andragogy with a similar bias in the other direction. I have coined the term – from the Greek 'gyn' and 'gogy' (literally the 'leading out of women') – as a signpost towards the need for a synthesis between the affective and the self-affirming. I believe that this offers a much more mature and creative analysis of an adulthood we might all wish to achieve. However, in the intervening space between the 'here and now' and the possible time when both sexes are indistinguishable in terms of societal constraints and dictats, I shall concentrate on elucidating the gynagogic model from the lessons to be learnt from women's articulation of *their* needs and goals.

Gendered Reflections

Memories contain the traces of the continuing process of appropriation of the social and the becoming, the constructing, of self. ... In their attempt to wrest meaning from the world, persons construct themselves; and in their struggle for intelligibility they reflect (Crawford et al., 1992).

The work of Crawford *et al.* has proved of enormous use in attempting to engage with the complexities of the reflective process. As I noted in the Introduction, 'the key to the heart of the MEC/APEL endeavour is the reflective process which will open the door to the learning derived from experience.' In terms of Kolb's 'learning cycle' – we experience, we reflect, we generalise and then we act – I have also noted that the process begs three basic questions:

- the concept of a unified subject enjoying equality of opportunity

- the concept of 'experience' as coherent, consistent and a site for rational intellectual excavation
- parity between the learning gained in one arena and the skills and competences demanded by another.

In Chapter 1 I discussed the problems inherent in the assumption of a unified 'I', and this chapter argues that women and men are socialised differently in terms of 'equality of opportunity'. I should now like to expand these issues in relation to assumptions regarding the coherence of experience.

At the beginning of the previous chapter, I argued that the 'crucial question for theorists and practitioners alike is how experience impacts upon the learner so that the knowledge gained can be retained and utilised in different contexts and in the future'. The proliferation of materials aimed at facilitating this process, including those published by The Learning From Experience Trust, the Open University and Macmillan, urge that the student begins the reclamation process by depicting the events of her life in some epistolary or diagrammatic form. She is urged to include painful events because they too provide rich sources from which learning may be extracted. This is not a surprising assumption. The belief that we understand through our suffering is the bedrock upon which some religious and psychoanalytic discourses are based.

But in order to extricate the learning gained and *be able to use it* — in order to complete the learning cycle – we have to be sufficiently distanced from the suffering so that rational reflection may take place. At its most basic, therefore, this approach is founded on the belief that our lives present linear journeys, and that chronological distance from significant emotional experiences will allow for the rational appraisal that the reflective process represents. Some practitioners acknowledge that there are risks attached. In Macmillan's *Profile Pack* (Brown *et al.*, 1995), students are reminded that they are:

> *concerned with the learning and not the experience itself. If you are still trying to 'cope' with the emotion, you are not in a position with this experience to articulate what you have learnt from it. Do not embark on reflection about emotionally*

*charged experiences if you have not already dealt with the
emotions that are likely to surface.*

Of course, this advice accords with our common-sense belief that 'time heals all', and in our own initial work with MEC
we debated the nature of our roles and responsibilities within
the learning environment. Were we educators or facilitators of a
therapeutic process? Most of us agreed with the advice echoed
by the *Profile Pack* authors and some of us, myself included, eschewed the 'lifeline' approach altogether, preferring to encourage our students to glean their learning and transferable skills
from 'safe' experiences such as previous jobs, community work
and domestic responsibilities.

In retrospect, I am astounded by my own naivety. Domestic
responsibilities do indeed furnish an enormous range of transferable skills, as Linda Butler (1993) has persuasively argued, as
long as we adhere to the andragogic model that 'adults are
what they have done'. But few would contest the fact that the
domestic or private realm is often the source of sustained pain
and conflict in terms of *who women are.*

In other words, if we base the MEC/APEL process upon
some form of andragogic – or self-directed – journey, then there
is every likelihood of eliciting a wide range of transferable
skills. However, this is not the same as facilitating a learning
process, if we are to regard learning as a dynamic intervention
involving critical analysis of the factors which combine to generate our understanding of who, and why, we are. I am not suggesting that the affective domain contains no potentially
transferable skills. Rather it is my contention that reflection is
not simply a vehicle for reclaiming learning from pain, neither
is it just a vehicle of cool appraisal for assessing the potential
for skills transferability. Although it can function as a medium
for both, I believe it is very often, and much more profoundly,
the cause of pain. And this is not in the sense of unearthing old
traumas but in the realisation of, and the connection with, the
implications around the initial painful event. Reflection can
thus call into being the deeper complexities in the formation of
experience and thence generate experience anew.

We surmise that the rewriting of childhood memories is not particularly helpful, whereas rewriting adult memories forces us to expose and question what we otherwise take for granted and enables experience, memory and hence the self to be reconstructed (Crawford et al., 1992).

Crawford *et al.* explore the implications of research undertaken into the nature of women's and men's memories. They base their methodology on the 'memory work' of the German feminist Frigga Haug. Their basic contention is that the 'self is socially constructed through reflection':

The underlying theory is that subjectively significant events, events which are remembered, and the way they are subsequently constructed, play an important part in the construction of self ... The initial data of the method, memory-work, are memories, which are reappraised collectively to uncover and document the social nature of their production.

Using their own memories, and those of groups of other women and men, the authors illustrated the discourses generated by social imperatives and the power that these discourses hold in the formation of our gendered selves. They use the term 'cliché' when describing the messages that our social imperatives convey. Their use is informed by Haug's explanation of the term: 'clichés condemn us to walk on the well-trodden path of what should be ... the cliché deliberates; it acts as an obstacle to understanding'. Thus the function of memory-work is to reveal the nature of the societal cliché and, where it hinders growth, to offer challenge.

In this sense, memory-work is reminiscent of consciousness-raising, which was such a feature of the early days of the women's movement. The difference lies in the degree of critical analysis which these women bring to bear on their findings. They are variously academics and psychologists, and they are well-versed in the complexities of recent feminist and post-structuralist debate. Their conceptual sophistication makes them unhappy with an essentialist view of the differences between the sexes. Yet, equally, they do not adhere to the more negative conclusions of some social constructionists. They do not wish to remain trapped in the supra-consciousness of their own fragmented selves and this is why they have much to offer educationalists. Without subscribing to the simplicity of the liberal/humanistic concept of the unified 'I' who can enjoy freedom of choice within the legal constraints imposed by society, they encourage the possibility of human agency; albeit within the limits of our 'circumscribed social space'.

However, in acknowledging the potential for change the authors do not underestimate the struggle that many of us must undergo; and their findings reiterate the gendered distinctions that I discussed above. They conclude that women are socialised in terms of their relations to others. They are 'burdened' with responsibility for maintaining the 'existing web of social relations'. In uncovering the 'clichés' that have formed our internalisation of these cultural imperatives, women may be enabled to effect change through redefinitions of their sense of self. But this may prove to be a very painful process:

> *In their troubled acceptance of the status quo and their resistance to its structures, women construct their anger, fear and pride, and other emotions. Such emotions are the markers of their resistance (Crawford et al., 1992).*

They are also gendered because they stem from gendered social imperatives. And if, as the authors conclude, reflection is essentially social, then I conclude that the reflective process is also a gendered process and will, of necessity, involve women in different struggles from men. This is why it is so important that the reflective process for women be undertaken in conjunction with others: 'we can change our own constructions, but change can be threatening, and so we need to do it together' (Crawford *et al.*, 1992).

This has obvious implications for the value of APEL programmes which are undertaken as distance (or sole) learning packages. There are two issues which need to be considered. The first needs no repetition; women need the support of other women if they are to unravel the 'clichés' which have constructed so many of their 'choices'. The second also has profound resonance for the nature of the educative process. For the conclusions that we are socially constructed in relation to others – and this is true of both men and women, although via different processes – means that our social re-construction should also be effected in conjunction with others. This would provide a means of challenging the polarity between dependence and autonomy. Neither need remain the special province of either sex, because 'autonomy and independence are paradoxically dependent upon others'. This is why I stated at the end of Chapter 1 that the learning process is ultimately a social process which can have profound social implications. And it is to the learning process in relation to women that I now turn.

'Experience' and the Learning Process

For Sally, integration entails being actively engaged in a learning process which involves actively relating to others, building on their contributions, and gently nurturing confidence. However, she and others often referred to the ways in which they could feel silenced by an intervention, often male – although few conceptualised it in gender terms, and virtually none in feminist terms (Warner Weil, 1989).

Given the preceding discussion, the fact that women might flourish in a learning environment which encouraged mutual support should come as no surprise. Warner Weil's work with mature returners was not conceived as a specific inquiry into the manner in which women and men might differently experience their return to education. However, the majority of her interviewees were women and she was able to offer some insights into possible gender differences. Of particular interest was the contrast between the women's comments and those of one of the men: 'Godfrey: When I am challenged and criticised by anyone, I feel every part of me is learning.' This is reminiscent of the discussion at the end of Chapter 1 which contrasted the findings of Belenky *et al.* with the genesis of Kolb's assumption that conflict was necessary for growth. At a deeper level this is undoubtedly true. We have seen that the reflective process for a woman involves unravelling the conflict, or tension, between her self defined in relation to others and her strivings for autonomy. But what is important in facilitating that process is that the facilitative or learning environment is not conflictual but the exact opposite. Societal challenges do not have to be replicated in the classroom in order to be overcome.

Of course there is nothing new in finding fault with the treatment of women in mainstream and higher education. But I would like to discuss one particular study because it speaks directly to the themes in this chapter.

The School for Independent Study at the former North East London Polytechnic incorporated student autobiography in its admission procedures for entry into its programme of self-defined courses. The process was laudable in design; its aim was to encourage students to use their own voices and experiences in forming their learning needs. 'However, even in a liberal environment like NELP, educational paradigms absorb radical intentions' (Humm, 1989). The problem lay in the fact that the rhetoric of the institution proved to be more in sympathy with the autobiographical discourse as presented by the men. The women's work suffered accordingly and fewer than 60 per cent of their autobiographies 'passed', compared with 80 per cent of the men's (Humm, 1989):

> Men made their lives into patterns of self-chosen events set in a rational pursuit of well-defined educational goals. Women's lives were always part of the lives of others ... These differences were echoed in the very syntax and vocabulary that men and women used. Women's voices were diffuse. Men already seemed to possess or to recognise the restricted mode of autobiographical discourse which tutors were happy to accept as a norm for course approval.

Rather than resign herself to an essentialist view of the nature of women's voices, Humm sought to understand the social constructions that would account for this disparity. She utilised the work of sociologist Pierre Bourdieu, who had analysed the discrepancy between the 'categories of experience' to which men and women have access:

> *Bourdieu conceives the social space of education to be a collection of fields of perception drawn from economics, culture, education and family background. He suggests that our power as agents in this space is increased by the number of positions we occupy in different fields, since the way we write or speak is the product of previous symbolic struggles. Many women students lack experience of the multiple sites of career, work and training. They occupy the domestic space described in their autobiographies and from that base their power in education is slighter than it might be. It is not that these lives are one-dimensional but the multiplicity in that site is not recognised. Women are, therefore, less likely to pass through any educational gate-keeping mechanism which closes off the field of the domestic (Humm, 1989).*

Humm also notes that 'men write autobiography as access to a future ... (women) prefer to retrieve a past'. Humm points to the Lacanian resonances in the manner in which the social processes which inform our subjectivities will also, and inevitably, determine the language with which we speak them. It is hardly surprising, therefore, that the autobiographies of the women in Humm's research 'exploit a rhetoric of uncertainty about themselves'; whereas those written by the men gave 'a positive and linear sense of identity'. This was consistent with the expectations and rhetoric of the institution; it is also consistent with the rhetoric implicit within the andragogical approach and the APEL process. Humm notes that NELP's assumptions were based upon '... a self-conscious "I" being able to perceive itself as the controller of its life history and social world.'

I wonder if at this point in the chapter, the reader shares with me the feeling that insisting on a constructionist approach to gender difference is all very well, but where are the opportunities for change? At the same time, she might also be thinking that her 'rhetoric' does not share the tentative quality noted above, or, at least, that she knows many women who express their needs and their goals with an assurance that many of the men in her acquaintance do not share. In a sense, the latter observation provides a response to the former.

There are indeed many women who enjoy access to a range of educational and vocational opportunities which were not available 20 years ago. This argues both for the possibilities of change and for the differences between women, which we must not overlook. If we are to pursue the gynagogic theme, then the fact that change is possible adds encouragement to our endeavours. But it also returns us to one of the main themes of the book. The fact that more women now operate in the 'public' sphere has done little to change the masculinist terms in which that sphere operates. If success in that realm, and the pursuit of autonomy, is predicated on a suppression of the affective then we have to be alert to the possible costs to women that such increased opportunities may bring.

This point was brought home to me in discussion with a colleague who is working on an in-depth enquiry into the desire for, and effects of, change among a group of mature returners. He and his colleague have utilised the narrative form as a means for students to make sense of their experiences through a series of intense one-to-one dialogues with the researchers. The work is ongoing but a preliminary finding casts an interesting sidelight on the experiences of Humm and her students. My colleague noted the comparison between the narrative of a female returner who had achieved comparative success in the public sphere with those of the men who had lost their space within it. Unsurprisingly, the woman wished to explore her motivation in terms of a linear progression towards enhanced future prospects. She was reluctant to engage in any 'affective' dialogue. Although the men did not have ready access to the affective realm in the initial stages of the project, their return visits to the researchers revealed an increasing awareness of the influence of the past and the need to make sense of their emotional relationship to it (Lea and West, 1994a/b; West, 1995). This aside is offered as an insight into the sacrifices that both genders are called upon to make in our existing polarities between the public and the private spheres. The fact that there is now more movement for women between the two has not resulted in significant changes in the ways in which those spheres are experienced or expressed.

So what are the implications for an educative process which seeks to 'make experience count'? The andragogic model upon which MEC/APEL is based can prove useful in eliciting the skills gained in one arena and highlighting their potential transferability. And it is understandable that students' recognition of the possible value of skills which they have hitherto taken for granted or denied could lead to enhanced self-confidence and greater self-esteem. However, I believe that most of the work undertaken in the field of MEC/APEL is conservative and reductionist, and serves to maintain the *status quo*. It amounts to little more than the reworking of the 'clichés' noted earlier and thus '(condemns) us to walk on the well-trodden path of what should be' (Crawford *et al.*, 1992).

If we are to embark upon an educative process which offers genuine possibilities for creative change, then we have to engage with the factors which constrain our understanding of *who, and why, we are*. My contention is that a process based upon gynagogic principles could offer just such possibilities. I now turn to an examination of what such a process might involve.

Notes Towards Gynagogy

One of the fundamental premises underpinning women's education, and certain other forms of experiential learning and adult education practice, has been the assumption that we should 'start from where the students are'. We are familiar with the commonplace injunction to 'begin with what the students know from their own experience and then move on to the general and theoretical implications'. It is a cornerstone of good facilitative practice. But we have already seen that the realm of the experiential is not simply a bedrock for rational excavation.

I have noted the inherent conservatism of the andragogic model, predicated on the liberal/humanist assumption of a unified and coherent 'I' enjoying equality of opportunity. On the contrary, I have agreed with those who have concluded that 'the self is no longer regarded as self-constitutive, but rather as a production of, variously, ideology, discourse, the structure of the unconscious and/or language' (Rothfield, 1990).

This conclusion has exacerbated the problem for feminists who are seeking to generate a transformative politics based on women's understanding of our experiences. At one extreme, Belsey has declared that: 'Experience must be the most unreliable source of theoretical production that we could possibly have chosen' (quoted by Gunew, 1990). This leaves us little room for manoeuvre. Rather more hopeful is the account given by de Lauretis (quoted by Gunew, 1990):

I should say from the outset that, by experience, I do not mean the mere registering of sensory data, or a purely mental (psychological) relation to objects and events, or the acquisition of skills and competences by accumulation or repeated exposure. I use the term not in the individualistic, idiosyncratic sense of something belonging to one and exclusively her own even though others might have 'similar' experiences; but rather in the general sense of a process by which, for all social beings, subjectivity is constructed ... It is the effect of that interaction – which I call experience; and ... is produced not by external ideals, values, or material causes, but by one's personal, subjective, engagement in the practices, discourses, and institutions that lend significance (value, meaning, and affect) to the events of the world.

Although the concluding sentiment does not elaborate upon the means of 'engagement' with the world, it allows for a measure of intervention into the realm of experience. It also allows a starting point for a gynagogic interweave between theory and practice:

1. Facilitators concerned with 'making experience count' – i.e. with a genuine educative process – must engage with the problems inherent in the ways that our multi-layered selves experience the world.
2. This, in turn, requires a supportive environment. Learning operates at the interface between the individual and the so-

cial. It is therefore a 'given' that MEC should operate as a group process in order to unravel the 'clichés' upon which our sense of our experiences is based.

3. Thus, the nature of our experiences are examined for traces of the broader discourses which inform them.

4. This means acknowledging the dynamic power of the reflective process.

5. New experiences will emerge as a result of the conflict between old assumptions and fresh understandings. This will generate a range of emotions, including anger and fear. These must not be exacerbated by pedagogic interventions such as 'challenge' and denial. They should be incorporated into the broader societal analysis in the hope of effecting change.

6. The need for 'women-only' provision should be accepted.

7. Funding must be made available for childcare, guidance and counselling.

8. The courses must be timed to fit in with domestic responsibilities.

Of course, I am merely reiterating what feminists and community and adult educators have been saying for years. Yet in proffering my own counter-terminology to the prevailing narrowly-defined educational discourse, I am adding another voice to the growing demand for an educative practice from which we could all benefit.

CHAPTER THREE

Skills and Competences, Learning and Education: In Pursuit of a Voice

Writing about the use of experience in adult learning requires the development of what Maudsley has called 'metalearning' – a theory of one's own learning providing a consequently greater awareness and control of the learning process. A crucial aspect of this is the use of personal experience, in particular the skill of reflecting on that experience (Usher, 1985).

This dichotomy between structure and action may also be reflected in the origins of the word 'education' itself. It is generally recognised that it may be derived from either one of two Latin words, 'educare' or 'educere': the first means 'to train' which implies to prepare a person to take their place within the structures of society, while the second means 'to draw out', which places more emphasis upon the person and the process (Jarvis, 1985).

Reason and Marshall (1987) suggest that when we set out on a process of self-discovery, we always get more than we bargained for. This suggests an open-endedness in terms of learning outcomes. What we learn is what we learn, not what we choose to learn, nor what we would have liked to have learnt. This is in contrast to some types of learning where situations are planned in order to bring about specific learnings (Brew, 1993).

There has been a considerable time-lapse between my writing the conclusion to the previous chapter and formulating this beginning to the next. Such a lapse, and the experiences of the author in the interim, should be of no consequence to the reader and would have remained unknown had I not brought attention to the fact. After all, this is a book purporting to deal with issues of educational relevance; the trials and tribulations of the writer in bringing this book to fruition are of no greater significance than the struggles undergone by anyone attempting to articulate their experiences within a particular framework and an agreed time-span. There is another factor which brings into question the relevance of a personal interjection at this point. This is not a novel. The reader is not enjoined by the chronology of the narrative to begin at page one and persevere conscientiously to the conclusion. Indeed, the likelihood is that this book will be skimmed and scanned until a section appeals to the interest of the individual. Anyone selecting this chapter from the contents page, and having read thus far, will probably be wondering what on earth this preamble has to do with the issues suggested by the title.

I had intended to provide a straightforward account of the current relationship between education and training with a view to situating MEC in one 'camp' or the other, or placing it at some point along a possible continuum between the two. My background reading soon revealed the folly in such an approach, whilst reinforcing what I had felt all along. The education/training debate is riven with contradiction, as are the discourses and policies which inform it. I then tried to thread my way through the wealth of material which has been written, in a further attempt to match the experience of facilitating MEC to a more or less coherent educational strategy. At this point life intervened and the process was put on hold until I could reclaim some degree of confidence in pursuing the task in hand.

In the course of this, I was once again struck by the similarity of my own position and that of the students on these courses. I have already noted that MEC is a 'double-edged sword':

> *It operates at the margins between our private and our public selves because it intervenes at the sites of self-disclosure, selection, relevance and control. In begging the question – 'count towards what?' – it can either 'cut the ties that bind'*

*or sever our connection to perhaps the most creative parts of
ourselves because they are not 'relevant'.*

My reading of the background materials was taking me further away from the emotional resonance of the process I was
pursuing. I was losing my voice in trying to re-articulate the
voices of others. I was also in danger of falsifying my own process of reflection by once again striving to adhere to the well-
worn academic pattern that carries its own heavily weighted
cultural imperative. In order to gain academic credibility I was
losing sight of the truth of my own experiences. The result was
an impasse – I felt compelled to continue accumulating pages of
notes from academic sources, yet I could not translate these into
the pages of my own chapter.

Then I read *Using Experience for Learning* (Boud *et al.*, 1993)
and, in turn, *experienced* the breakthrough that I needed. The
courage that the contributors to the volume showed in exploring their own struggles in articulating their learning processes
encouraged me to come to terms with my own. What follows
are my reflections upon that struggle.

In recent months I have attended several meetings which
were concerned with the issues relating to assessing learning
'outcomes'. I shall give a brief account of two of them. The first
was held at the WEA national office in London and was convened in order to introduce the results of a commissioned project to examine and elucidate 'learning outcomes within the
WEA's liberal programme' (Daines, 1994). There were two reasons why the project was initiated. The whole area of quality
assurance is high on the list of educational priorities, whoever
the provider. The discrete nature of WEA provision, residing as
it does within relatively autonomous Districts, has militated
against any systematic assessment of quality control at the national level. Yet we are a national organisation, and regarded as
such by the Further Education Funding Council (FEFC), which
provides approximately half our funding. We are also in the
somewhat anomalous position of having retained a significant
amount of financial support in order to continue providing liberal education which is not accredited. It was of crucial importance, therefore, to be able to persuade the funding body that

our liberal adult education programmes have a sound educational base and that we engender learning that is worth the financial investment that the FEFC accords it. (It has to be noted that this funding also supports the WEA's infrastructure and not just our courses.)

But how were we to assess the merits of our provision? How were we to translate our notions of value into a currency which would enable us to continue trading in the educational market-place? The answer, of course, and one familiar to all educationalists in whatever field, was 'outcomes'. So we addressed ourselves to the question 'how were we to express the learning experiences our students undergo in terms of measurable outcomes?'.

Once again, the WEA found itself in a somewhat contradictory position. On the one hand, there were those within both the voluntary movement and the professional staff who regarded such a move as anathema to the spirit of the organisation. On the other hand, there were those who remembered the tutorial class system, when rigorous assessment procedures were an integral part of the WEA's claim to academic excellence as well as providing an, albeit informal, access route to higher education (WEA *1918 Yearbook*; WEA *1919 Report*; Tawney, 1953).

Daines and the steering group were acutely aware of the sensibilities of the part-time tutors and the voluntary movement and had produced a document which 'refocused interest from *assessment* of learning to its *description*', in close liaison with a few field staff and student members:

> *Though it may not be feasible to summatively assess learning in the context of a WEA class, an alternative and, it is to be hoped,* acceptable means of demonstrating that worthwhile learning takes place in WEA courses *does exist. Intended learning could be explicitly planned for with clearly identified aims and learning objectives, and formally agreed with students at the commencement of a course. At the end of the course, the learning which has taken place could be identified and* described *by students, and confirmed by tutors, as their achieved learning outcomes.*

This may be defined as a mutually-agreed learning contract between tutor and students, whose fulfilment is describable by both parties. *Such an approach should accommodate the political raison d'etre of the WEA and the quite proper concern of all those interested in learning outcomes, not least our funders (Daines, 1994, original emphasises).*

The emphasis on *describing* learning rather than assessing it was intended as a means of providing a system of measurement which would at the same time safeguard the breadth and range of learning which might be engendered within a WEA class. Indeed, the students' final evaluation form asked for the inclusion of 'personal learning outcomes' in order to accommodate the serendipitous, idiosyncratic and unintended learning in terms of the original learning contract.

Prior to the meeting, participants had been sent tutor guidelines and asked to formulate the learning outcomes for one of the courses which we teach. The guidelines were quite clear. There were two stipulations to which we should adhere. The 'outcomes' were to be introduced with the phrase: 'at the end of the course you should be able to ...'; and we were to couch the learning objectives in the terms provided and which follow here:

Words which can be used when writing learning objectives:

Knowledge

define	write	underline
state	recall	select
list	recognize	reproduce
name	label	measure

Comprehension

identify	illustrate	explain
justify	represent	judge
select	name	contrast
indicate	formulate	classify

Application

predict	choose	construct
select	find	compute
assess	show	use
explain	demonstrate	perform

Analysis

analyze	select	justify
identify	separate	resolve
conclude	compare	criticize

Synthesis

combine	argue	select
restate	discuss	relate
summarize	organize	generalize
precis	derive	conclude

Evaluation

judge	support	identify
evaluate	defend	avoid
determine	attack	select
recognize	criticize	choose

Receiving

listen	accept	identify
attend	receive	favour
prefer	perceive	select

Responding

state	select	record
answer	list	develop
complete	write	derive

Value

accept	increase	indicate
recognize	develop	decide
participate	attain	influence

Organization

organize	find	associate
judge	determine	form
relate	correlate	select

Words which should be avoided when writing learning objectives:

know	appreciate	understand
be aware of	really know	really understand
be familiar with	have a working knowledge of	
have a good grasp of	realize the significance of	

Readers familiar with Bloom's taxonomy (see Bloom *et al.*, 1956) will recognise the similarities with these formulations, and those who have used *A Learner's Introduction to Building on Your Experience* (Buckle, 1988) will also note that the first six categories are identical to the levels of learning listed there on pages 31–36, and discussed in Chapter 9 of this volume.

What is interesting about these authors' uses of the taxonomy is their distinction between knowledge, and ability or competence. Buckle elucidates the distinction in two columns; one is headed 'what you know' and the other 'what you can do'. 'Understanding' is included in the first column, which is concerned with knowledge, whilst the second column outlines the capabilities to which such understanding leads. This column is couched solely in terms of 'action' verbs. It is also interesting to note that the role of 'understanding' is utilised only at the lower levels (2 and 3) of the learning process, which are concerned with knowledge 'interpretation' and 'application'.

Given that Daines is following a similar model and that he is attempting to elucidate 'outcomes', it is not surprising that his taxonomy is concerned with 'capabilities', that is with 'action' verbs, and that he asks us to eschew the role of 'understanding' from the outset. In other words, he is not concerned with the (private) depth or apprehension of the knowledge acquired in the learning process, but with its (public) utilisation in terms of competence and ability.

At the time, my teaching commitment was in training tutors to facilitate our MEC programmes. I attempted, therefore, to articulate the learning outcomes which should result from participation in the tutor-training courses. The following is my attempt to adhere to Daines' guidelines:

Make Your Experience Count:
Tutor Training Course

Times: 10.30–4.30

No. of Meetings: 5

The aim of this course is to familiarise potential MEC tutors with the process, methods, theoretical background and pedagogical implementation of a WEA/MEC course. It will include an examination of the problems and pitfalls that may occur and suggest ways of dealing with them. This course utilises experiential approaches to learning and seeks to familiarise tutors with some of the issues their students will encounter.

As a result of this course you should be able to:

- facilitate a WEA/MEC course

- explain the principles of MEC to your students

- analyse the relationship between the theoretical underpinning to MEC and its practical implementation

- recognise the pitfalls and problems

- select the most appropriate ways of dealing with group and individual issues which arise during the course

- evaluate your own and the group's progress, process and 'outcomes' at the end of the course.

(I was unhappy with the use of 'issues' and 'encounter' because they failed to express the dynamic impact the process so often entailed.) I was not the only participant who found the process to be a struggle. Some of my colleagues, representing a wide range of subject areas, also spoke of the limiting nature of the exercise. We felt constrained by *our awareness* of the difference between our conception of what the learning process entailed and the action verbs available to describe the outcomes. Once again, we experienced the difference between process and product. Sharing feedback with a colleague elicited the same response: this might describe what we, as tutors, and the students do; it does not reflect the myriad intersections through which learning actually impacts upon the learner nor the complexities inherent in those encounters. It fails to *describe* what happens. There is a clear distinction between process and outcome in exactly the same way that there is between apprehension and competence, although, in both cases, the two may overlap. To argue that we can describe the learning that takes place in WEA classes in terms of the outcomes that accrue is to elucidate only half of the equation. And yet the discourse in which the 'outcomes' debate is articulated is increasingly denying that such an absence exists by arguing vociferously that all worthwhile learning can be couched in terms of outcomes if we only put our minds to it.

There was a further factor which added to my anxiety. I have already noted that the WEA students' final evaluation form asked for the inclusion of 'personal learning outcomes' in order to give space for the effects of the learning experience which had not been articulated as part of the course's aims and outcomes. Daines admitted that none of the students in the pilot project had included anything other than a re-write of the aims and outcomes specified at the outset. I could only conclude that the discourse of the learning 'contract' had effectively delineated the parameters within which the experiences of the courses might be described. Any others which did not fall within the remit specified did not warrant inclusion because, by implication, they would not be valid.

The second event was held at the University of Kent, with senior colleagues from the School of Continuing Education (SCE), the Kent Adult Education Service (KAES) and the WEA. The meeting had been called to examine some of the ways in which learning may be assessed. It had been prompted by the Higher Education Funding Council for England (HEFCE) circular detailing the forthcoming changes in the funding arrangements for continuing education departments in universities.

Ring-fenced funding for non-accredited liberal provision in continuing education departments would cease in 1995. Although some money would remain available for such provision, it was obvious to all that the majority of courses would have to carry some form of accreditation. The SCE was exploring with WEA and LEA colleagues how best to effect the changes to our joint programme with the minimum harm to the existing student body, most of whom, it was felt, would baulk at the concept of studying for credit as opposed to 'for learning's own sake'.

The SCE wished to explore the WEA's 'learning outcomes' project to assess its applicability to their own accreditation procedures. They also wished to share the results of the pilot stage of the implementation of their Regional Awards Scheme (RAS). This provided one means by which students could utilise the learning gained on liberal courses and translate it into credit towards SCE certificates and diplomas. It was, in effect, a scheme for accrediting prior learning.

Our WEA colleague spoke first. She had been a member of the 'learning outcomes' steering group, and provided a full account of the project's inception, process and recommendations. Her talk was greeted with interest. Yet it soon became clear that the project's insistence on describing rather than *assessing* outcomes rendered it of little use in terms of the School's need to provide a means of articulating the latter. What was fascinating about the discussion was the degree to which the WEA's discourse and the School's were becoming polarised. Considering the anxiety of many WEA colleagues, at the meeting in London, about the reductionism of the 'learning outcomes' model, it was revealing to discover its apparent irrelevance to any stringent assessment process.

The disparity between our discourses became more apparent in our discussions regarding the RAS. This had been conceived as a method for acknowledging prior learning by translating it into competences recognised in HE. Once again, we were introduced to a taxonomy of learning outcomes which was reminiscent of Bloom. This, at least, was shared with the WEA model. However, the rigour attached to the transformation process caused disquiet among the WEA participants, myself included. There were two basic issues. On the one hand, the School was concerned to prove the academic acceptability of its model by adhering to a strict template delineating parity and equivalence with the competences expected at HE Level One. Adult learners on our joint liberal programmes had to show that they could match up to the standards required by the academy. Whilst we in the WEA argued that many of our courses were at least equivalent to Level One, we baulked at what we perceived to be another reductionism in the way such parity could be expressed. What the RAS model offered was a thorough-going assessment of equivalence; our anxiety was that it represented a re-working of the academic *status quo* and, therefore, sadly, could not address the potential it was once proclaimed lay inherent in APL for challenging the discourse of the academy.

I was reminded of research I had undertaken into 'learner managed learning' (LML) the previous year. Then I had concluded that:

> If LML is regarded as an 'achieved state' rather than a 'process of becoming' then it will only have relevance to students who have already succeeded within the academic mainstream (Fraser, 1993).

I felt that the RAS model represented another proof of this conclusion. It seemed to concentrate on the 'achieved state' of HE Level One, and therefore demanded such a rigorous translation process that it would limit accessibility to its promise as an alternative access route, and thence to its claim that it could 'recognise' prior learning. Once again, the breadth of experience had to be shaped and trimmed, selected and reworked to fit an existing model.

The other interesting facet of our discussions at the meeting at the University was a comment from one colleague who noted that the RAS model shared similarities with the competence models being proposed through General National Vocational Qualifications (GNVQs). Another colleague, who has worked extensively with a variety of credit mechanisms within HE, then proclaimed that such similarities proved that 'we were pursuing the right model', otherwise the various competence schemes would have been at variance and produced differing outcomes. I argued, on the contrary, that the similarity in outcomes was simply the result of the fact that all the models shared the same basic frame of reference and thus the outcomes were predetermined by the limits of the framework.

The sadness that clung to some of us at the end of the meeting was not a result of the disagreements that had taken place. We had crossed swords before on several occasions but had always known that the breaches would be healed because we enjoyed a close working relationship and knew that we were working for the same ends and within the same tradition. It seemed to me at that meeting that the days of that relationship were numbered. The School had no choice but to follow the routes that the funding circular seemed to dictate. Perhaps we, in the WEA, were simply luxuriating in what remained of our own relative freedom until our own funding restrictions might force us to pursue those same pathways. There is no doubt some truth in this accusation. But what are the consequences of this? Just as the students on the 'learning outcomes' project would not speak of their own process outwith the limits of the discourse made available to them, we had experienced the irrelevance of arguing for a greater potentiality within the models being adopted by the School. Once again, the parameters were being set within which experiences must be constrained and contained, and we could only lament the passing of a space in which such potentialities would not have been perceived as indulgent and redundant.

I explained at the beginning of this chapter that my experiences between concluding the previous section and beginning this one had rendered me silent until I could find the courage to articulate their resonance within this work as a whole. I have included this description of these two meetings because the effects they engendered reflected my own sense of the increasing limits to the sayable. My basic contention is that the relentless translation of the learning process to the narrow reductionism of the 'outcomes' model throughout the education system is effectively silencing whole sections within the orchestras which play the harmonies *and discords* making up the complexities which comprise our 'selves'. *Education* is being subsumed within the *training* discourse (Raggatt and Unwin, 1991; Thorpe *et al.*, 1993; Edwards *et al.*, 1993) and the flutes of resistance are being drowned by the relentless drum of the vocational 'need' for flexibility, adaptability and the entrepreneurial.

There is nothing new in this, and before I am accused of na-ive idealism, I should like to point out that the same debate was a feature of educational policy-making at the end of the last century. The development of Goldsmiths' College serves as il-lustration of my argument. As Firth notes (1991), its original function as Goldsmiths' Company's Technical and Recreative Institute in 1891 was:

> *the promotion of the individual skill, general knowledge, health and well-being of young men and women belonging to the industrial, working and poorer classes.*

And Firth notes the political and economic imperatives which provided the Institute's raison d'etre:

> *there were strong public and parliamentary feelings that Britain was falling behind other countries, particularly Germany, in the provision of cheap scientific and technical education.*

How does this differ from our current preoccupation with the supposed needs and demands of the workplace? It is cer-tainly undeniable that higher education has become available to a larger number of the population but has the social engineer-ing which has effected the sea-change had any measurable ef-fect on the quality of provision which greater numbers enjoy?

I have noted elsewhere (Fraser, 1993) that the university system is growing faster than at any time since the Middle Ages. At the end of the 1980s there were, for example, 250,000 full-time students in 83 universities. Five years later there are an estimated 750,000 in 123 universities in the UK. Although there are a number of reasons for this increase, the most important in terms of state intervention has been a *broad* political consensus that our education system had consistently failed to equip sufficient people to deal with the demands of our advanced economy. Britain was ranked thirteenth in the 'world competitiveness scoreboard' in 1992, with Japan and Germany holding first and second places (Rajan, 1991). It was deemed necessary to encourage greater access to educational opportunity and to foster a closer elision between academic and vocational pursuits. Rajan notes that:

> *As businesses develop a quality and competitiveness culture, they need people with flexibility and innovative ability, as well as basic technical competence ... Their education and training will need to be broadly based, promoting not just narrow technical understanding of the job, but competence in broader skills which generate adaptability, responsibility for standards, creativity and the flexibility to respond to changing demand.*

To this end, the Confederation of British Industries (CBI) launched a series of National Targets for Education and Training in 1991 after consultation with 78 organisations including educationalists, employers, Training and Enterprise Councils (TECs), the Trades Union Congress, the Department for Education and the Department of Employment. National Targets have been divided into two categories – lifetime learning targets and foundation learning targets. They have recently been revised as follows:

Lifetime Learning Targets for 2000:

1. 60 per cent of the workforce to be qualified to NVQ level 3, Advanced GNVQ or 2 GCE A-level standard.

2. 30 per cent of the workforce to have a vocational, professional, management or academic qualification at NVQ level 4 or above.

3. 70 per cent of all organisations employing 200 or more employees, and 35 per cent of those employing 50 or more, to be recognised as Investors in People.

Foundation Learning Targets for 2000:

1. By age 19, 85 per cent of young people to achieve 5 GCSEs at grade C or above, an Intermediate GNVQ or an NVQ level 2.

2. 75 per cent of young people to achieve level 2 competence in communication, numeracy and IT by age 19; and 35 per cent to achieve level 3 competence in these core skills by age 21.

3. By age 21, 60% of young people to achieve 2 GCE A-levels, and advanced GNVQ or an NVQ level 3.

Does it really matter that NVQs are now being criticised by some for their failure to address the 'needs of the economy'? Should we note, with no little irony, that their place in the broader economic picture has not transformed our position vis-à-vis our competitors in Europe and that we remain in the same relation to the German 'threat' that we did at the turn of the century?

> *Indeed, some (Jarvis and Prais, 1989: 70) have argued that many of the NVQs being specified by British employers target such low skill levels that they run the risk of producing a 'certified semi-literate under-class'... In this respect, the contrast offered by Lane (1988) between the ways in which British and German employers have been changing production technologies, work organisations, and skill requirements, is illuminating (Keep, 1993).*

The questions are obviously rhetorical. I am arguing for a different space in which to articulate the educational discourse. The problem resides in the perennial debate about the nature and purpose of 'education': how we articulate that debate lies, in turn, in the language available to us. The tragedy of our current situation is that there is little space in which to foster an alternative.

I am aware that I am speaking 'from the margins' and that this argument no longer enjoys the currency that it had in the 1970s or early 80s. Such marginal discourses are criticised, if they are noticed at all, for their irrelevance to contemporary imperatives. But we need to encourage a wider social debate which includes:

> The new social movements [which] challenge the very privileging of rational-technical thinking over and above creativity, imagination and feeling. These lend themselves to informal and reciprocal forms of learning, experienced as discovery rather than transmission, and characterized by self-management rather than external validation (Field, 1991).

It is within this alternative discourse introduced by Field that I would wish to place the potentiality of our MEC programmes. It is a wish which is reflected in the following lines from a poem entitled 'Humility' (Sorley Maclean, from *Spring Tide and Neap Tide: Selected poems 1932–72*), a poem which itself comes from the margins:

Fhuar mi faoisgneadh as a' chocull
a rinn cor mo reis
is dhiuchd barr-guc m' anama
bho arraban 'na leig.

I have burst from the husk
which my life's condition imposed,
and my spirit's blossom has come
out of distress an adamant.

I noted early in this chapter that I had 'lost my voice' and could not break the impasse that prevailed between echoing others' voices and claiming my own. Then, I stated, that I had *experienced* the breakthrough that I needed by reading *Using Experience for Learning* (Boud *et al.*, 1993). If I am to reflect on the learning that I gained from that reading then I have to engage with the process that my use of the word 'experience' entailed:

> The way in which we interpret experience is intimately connected with how we view ourselves. Developing confidence and building self-esteem both flow from, and are

necessary for, learning from experience. If we do not respect our perceptions and have confidence in what we see and feel, then we cannot make use of the information which we garner from the world. A belief in our ability to act and learn is a prerequisite for learning; without this we are passive participants in the constructs of others (Boud et al., 1993).

Events in my personal life had reduced my self-confidence to such a low ebb that for several months I felt that I was performing as an automaton. In other words, I kept on working and attending meetings, such as those described above, but I was always accompanied by the conviction that I was not really 'there'. This is not to say that I was unable to learn during this period, in the sense that I was continuing to 'garner information' and could organise it in a way to broaden my understanding of the issues involved. But I was plagued with doubts. We internalise our knowledge of the world in a manner which is consistent with our world-view. If that view is jaundiced and fragile then how do we know that we are 'seeing' anything other than a reflection of our own fragility?

The meetings reinforced my sense of isolation. In each case, the authority of the discourse lay with those who had assessed the situation and were trying to implement the changes deemed necessary in order to safeguard future funding. The need for such pragmatism, dictated from above, in other words the funding bodies, clearly delineated the relevant limits to the sayable. This is not to suggest that other views were not heard, but it felt as if they were regarded with the same sort of indulgence that is reserved for those who are out of touch and have lost their grasp on reality. I fully acknowledge that this was the feeling that I had about myself and so I may simply have been projecting my negativity on to the proceedings. But the problem with not 'knowing' whether or not this was the case merely compounded the depth of my anxiety and alienation.

I was also, throughout this time, unable to write. I could still learn in the sense that I was able to extract information from other sources and add to my knowledge stock. I could 'make sense' of the learning in terms of being able to understand the words I was reading but I couldn't respond to them. I couldn't speak to them – there was no internalised dialogue and therefore I was silent. I felt I could no longer act in the world and so retreated to the safety of habit and repetition. My personal experiences, and the learning I had gleaned and then utilised in coping with them, had diminished me. What use was my ability to rationalise my situation when I couldn't effect any change? What good was my cognitive apprehension of 'crises in adulthood' when I was trapped in one of my own?

For several weeks I was convinced that my experiences counted for little. During this period I was most susceptible to the voices, and authority, of others. I needed a world of absolutes and imperatives, of simplicity and order. Thankfully, my friends, family and colleagues resisted my facile appeals for certainties and, rather, shared more of their own doubts and insecurities. By treasuring these fragilities, I began to hold less contempt for my own. I am still collecting the fragments and I am aware that the process of ordering them will be a long one. I am also aware that the picture which is emerging is not the one I had before and that I can predict neither its shape or colour nor my relationship to it. These are 'outcomes' which no learning contract could ever delineate:

> *Wisdom may come through experience, but it does not come through an accumulation of experience. Unlearning is about being prepared to throw out what one has learnt and begin afresh. I'm inclined to say that it is the process of learning that is important; that there is only the journey, never the destination. However, I think what I am referring to is the process of unlearning: the attempt to access our inner knowings; the coming face to face, again and again, with our ignorance; with our not-knowing. The highest point of knowing is not knowing. Herein lies the paradox of learning from experience (Brew, 1993).*

If I had read these words a month before, they would have meant nothing to me. I had to reach the point where my own re-ordering allowed me to recognise the truth of these words in relation to my own process. This is what I meant when I said that I *experienced* the breakthrough that I needed. It was not merely a question of cognitive appraisal. Neither was the experience something that 'happened' to me. In the rest of her chapter, Brew talks of the failure of our conventional educational practices to aid her striving towards 'inner-knowing'. In articulating her struggles, she encouraged me to describe my own.

What conclusions may be drawn from this chapter? None that I am prepared to elucidate. I could list the lessons I have learnt from my experiences but what would be the point? Each reader will take from this encounter exactly as much or as little as necessary and I cannot dictate those 'outcomes'.

I would simply like to point out in closing that there were two reasons why I chose to speak so personally in this chapter. This volume is concerned with Making Experience Count. Until I had come to terms with my own battles, I felt that I would be acting in 'bad faith' in terms of the rest of the project. This conviction was reinforced by the feeling I often have that books purporting to deal with 'learning processes' or 'adult developmental cycles' tend to talk as if our students are a different species from us who write of them. *Their* experiences become material for *our* disquisitions; and they, in turn, become the objects of our subjective scrutiny. This is part of the distancing process which compartmentalises our educational discourse into the elements of influence dictated by policy-makers and government quangos. This is why we talk of 'skills and competences, education and training'. It is only when we adopt a holistic approach to our educative endeavours that we will be able to acknowledge the 'educere' element. It is only then that we shall be able to respond to the plea encapsulated in the following poem by John Wood (from *How Do You Feel? A guide to your emotions,* Prentice-Hall Inc., 1974). It is only then that we shall be justified in facilitating the process wherein our students are enabled to make sense of their experiences in active encounters predicated upon mutual respect and trust.

Poem for Everyman *(sic)*

I will present you
parts
of
my
self
slowly
if you are patient and tender.
I will open drawers
that mostly stay closed
and bring out places and people and things
sounds and smells, loves and frustrations, hopes and sadnesses
bits and pieces of three decades of life
that have been grabbed off
in chunks
and found lying in my hands.
they have eaten
their way into my memory
carved their way into my
heart
altogether – you or i will never see them –
they are me.
if you regard them lightly
deny that they are important
or worse, judge them
i will quietly, slowly
begin to wrap them up,
in small pieces of velvet,
like worn silver and gold jewelry,
tuck them away
in a small wooden chest of drawers

and close.

Only Connect

An honourable human relationship – that is, one in which two people have the right to use the word 'love' – is a process, delicate, violent, often terrifying to both persons involved, a process of refining the truths they can tell each other.

It is important to do this because it breaks down human self-delusion and isolation.

It is important to do this because in so doing we do justice to our own complexity.

It is important to do this because we can count on so few people to go that hard way with us.

On Lies, Secrets, Silence, *Adrienne Rich, 1980, Virago.*

This section deals with the six pilot MEC courses that we ran in the South Eastern District of the WEA between 1991 and 1992. The discussion begins with an account of the recruitment and training of the project team. It then examines the process of each of the courses from both the tutors' and the students' points of view.

It is important to explain how the material for this section was developed. Originally, this book was perceived as a collective enterprise. This was consistent with our political, and educational, belief that one single voice should not be seen as having authority over the experiences of others; although it was agreed that I should furnish the 'introduction' and 'conclusion' for the simple reason that I had overall responsibility for the project and had already facilitated MEC courses.

In order to be true to the nature of our endeavour, we did not want to pre-empt the 'outcomes' of the accounts by organising our material in relation to the issues and debates which we assumed were central but might prove otherwise as the programmes unfolded. In other words, we had the broadest possible agenda: write about what happened and the sense we made of that experience. We then met to discuss each other's work and the issues that had arisen. At this point the problems inherent in our approach became apparent.

(a) We had all assumed that the diversity of our student groups would furnish sufficiently distinct material to retain the interest of the reader. At the same time, the issues which we predicted would arise were, indeed, at the forefront of all of our accounts: problems of student motivation and lack of confidence, of time constraints, of the validity of our programmes in relation to the public arena. Our chapters therefore had a 'sameness' which was not offset by our individual voices nor by the differences in our 'target' groups.

(b) The differences in our accounts were also a problem. In using the written word as a medium for our experiences, we each adopted the register with which we were most familiar. Thus our chapters spanned the spectrum from the most intensely personal and confessional to the much more 'objective' academic analysis. We worried that some of our work spoke more of our 'selves' than of the processes of the students on our courses. We were concerned that our personal idiosyncrasies were 'getting in the way' of the purpose of our project and would therefore render our conclusions suspect, if not totally indulgent.

(c) This issue of mediation presented another problem. Our accounts also varied in the degree to which they spoke of specific as opposed to general student concerns. This raised the question of how to respect individual confidentiality. It also highlighted the equally difficult dilemma concerning the degree to which we were appropriating our students' experiences as material for our own discussions. They were in danger of becoming the objects of our scrutiny. One of the team was so concerned about the implications of this that she refused to submit an account of her course. She argued that the only moral solution was to allow the students to write their own chapter; otherwise we were all potentially guilty of speaking for others, thus, at best, mistranslating their 'realities', if not actually censoring or silencing them.

We knew that we would have to re-write some of our accounts in an attempt to address these issues. But we had a deadline to meet and our working schedules prevented us from devoting sufficient time to agree upon solutions to these problems. The document that we submitted was greeted with warmth and encouragement but it had failed to 'match up' to the promise outlined in our abstract. Our material was too diverse to constitute a sustainable narrative. It would have to be reworked, with one voice assuming responsibility. After further discussions with the team and the publisher, it was agreed that I should be charged with this task.

I am aware of the irony surrounding this 'outcome'. Considering our failure to address the issues described above, I was then placed in the position of possibly repeating that failure by mediating both students' and tutors' experiences via the register with which I feel most comfortable. What follows is therefore my understanding of the tutors' accounts placed within the thematic frameworks which I have discussed in Section 1. The organising principle has been my attempt to illustrate the problems inherent in facilitating MEC by utilising the 'relevant' elements from the tutors' original narratives. In some cases, I have utilised the tutor's (or tutors') own words; in others, I have chosen to use the words of the students. This decision was based upon the material I had at my disposal and in an attempt to give equal voice to all the participants on the programmes. I have to stress that in every case where the words of the students are quoted verbatim, we secured permission beforehand.

My intention is that each of the following chapters reflects upon one or more of our basic concerns, which I have already summarised as cohering around MEC/APEL's assumption of:

- the concept of a unified subject enjoying equality of opportunity
- the concept of 'experience' as coherent, consistent and a site for rational intellectual excavation
- parity between learning gained in one arena and the skills and competences demanded by another.

However, each of the chapters has its own introduction, with more specific questions to address. In some cases, I have added comments of my own. In others, I have presented the material 'as it stands', without further reference to the issues under discussion. This is deliberate. This book is about the problems that a particular team of tutors found they had to address in dealing with a specific educational agenda. Given that our responses are bound to refer to the political and gendered positions which we have adopted or inherited, it would be antithetical to the nature of our project to maintain our insistence upon the way our findings are interpreted by the reader. The tutors' and students' 'narratives' are as open to debate as the novel, and should be 'read' with an equivalent constructively critical stance.

CHAPTER FOUR

Recruitment and Training

Knowledge is an experience and not a formula (D.H. Lawrence).

Recruitment

Part of the WEA monies had been set aside for training purposes. It was important to establish a network of tutors for two reasons. As far as I knew at the time, I was the only tutor in the District working within the area of MEC/APEL. (This later proved not to be the case.) And so we needed new tutors. We also needed to establish a network. I have already pointed out that one of the paradoxical strengths of the WEA is its marginality. Because we were excluded from certain funding sources and accredited bodies, we had worked extensively at forging links, both formally and informally, with other providers: educational guidance services, employers, social services, etc. This would prove of immense value to our students if we could operate within a supportive network and share our contacts. It would also provide a source of comfort and encouragement to the team itself as the project progressed.

It was therefore decided to recruit tutors from areas within our provision which already operated on the margins and which demanded initiative and commitment. As it happened, when word got round we had applications from two tutors in WEA London District and so our first gathering comprised:

- two part-time tutors from Brighton Women's Education Branch
- two part-time tutors in assertiveness and new opportunities for women

- two mature 'returners' – one working within the field of 'Return to Learn' courses; the other was beginning her teaching career and had attended several women's studies courses
- three other part-time tutors within academic feminism
- one (male) part-time WEA Organiser from the London District who worked in community education
- one (female) part-time tutor, from the London/Essex region who also specialised in women's education.

My colleague, the Tutor Organiser responsible for training in the WEA South Eastern District, also attended the first session.

Training

The training programme was held over a period of four full days. Most of the materials used were those available from The Learning From Experience Trust. Others included readings from *Making Sense of Experiential Learning* (Warner Weil and McGill, 1989), extracts from *Adults Learning* and my own jigsaw reading exercise. (For the handouts, see bibliography.)

The Aims

The overriding aim was to familiarise existing WEA tutors with the concept, methodology and contradictions in teaching or facilitating MEC/APEL courses. Thus, the days were planned as follows:

- Day 1: Experiential immersion in experiential learning as process and content
- Day 2: Theoretical and applicable use of APEL in HE
- Day 3: APEL and the WEA ethos: the 'four villages'
- Day 4: NVQs and the planning of our own programmes.

Content

Day 1: After my welcome, the tutor/students were paired to elicit basic introductions and current interest in and knowledge of APEL. They then fed back to the whole group. As I suspected, most of the tutors had heard little about APEL and declared themselves 'ignorant but willing to learn'. I had already decided to conduct the day as if it were the commencement of a new MEC course. Thus the tutors would be immersed experientially from the outset and gain knowledge of the materials and processes by actually working through them.

I made it quite clear that my 'expertise' was limited, and that all I was offering was an introduction to the process as I perceived it. They were to take as much or as little as would suit their own facilitative styles. Thus, conscious of the need to adopt two evaluative roles – as prospective tutor and as current student – we embarked on our task.

The process of 'Making Experience Count' requires that we learn:

How to look at what we have learned in our lives and make sense of it.

This forms the basis of a typical MEC course if we break it down into its component parts:

- what is experiential learning?
- how do we recognise and validate it?
- how do we own that process for ourselves?
- how do we utilise it in the future? Should we complete a portfolio? What currency would it have?

We began by brainstorming on the board, and then individually noted down the differences we perceived between formal and informal learning. These were written up as two columns, and the personal nature of much informal learning soon became evident. This led us to the problem of recognition, validation and ownership and the tension between the publicly acceptable and the uniquely personal.

Firstly the 'students' worked through a confidence-building exercise individually (Handout 1). They then worked in twos for mutual encouragement, validation and to prompt other thoughts. All of them were then asked to feed back their completed lists of 'achievements' on the board. I stressed that it was important not to exclude the more reticent contributor: the more material on the board, the more powerful the sense of personal and group accomplishment. We paused for a review of the material thus far. I comment on the response in the section on course evaluation.

We continued with a discussion concerning the undeniable fact that much experiential learning is derived from painful and traumatic life events. Some facilitators of MEC programmes begin their courses with students drawing and 'feeling' their lifelines. We discussed the implications of this approach.

It was important to reiterate the length of the process involved in a course of this kind. We discussed Handout 2 and noted that a typical MEC programme usually runs for 15 weeks at three hours per week. (The fact that our own funding constraints dictated a 10–12-week course of two to two-and-a-half hours per week was to have repercussions, as the following chapters illustrate.)

In the afternoon we reconvened to meet the dilemma of how to progress from:

> What I Did > What I Learnt > Possible General Competences

Handout 3 was discussed within the large group and it was acknowledged that the categories had to be broken down further if the process was to be genuinely meaningful and not merely a glib exercise. We discussed the more complex example, which categorised the process in the following way (Handout 4):

Activity > What I Did > Knowledge Used >
Skills Used > Competence Statements >
Possible General Competences

The 'students' then chose one event from their own list of experiences and described it in the terms of the new categories. This was once again shared with a partner, and then one of them volunteered to share theirs with the whole group.

We paused for a further review. There was concern that the further breakdown into knowledge and skills might have facilitated the exercise but did not do justice to the complexity of the learning process. The 'students' found the progression from 'What I Did' to 'What I Learnt' to 'Possible General Competences' more comfortable to work with.

The group was then given a further handout (Handout 5) describing interest in terms of occupational clusters which would help their own students explore possible future directions. The day was then evaluated in plenary.

Day 2: The intention on the second day was to examine APEL's potential as a fast-route access course into HE. Once again, the tutors were to explore the implications from the point of view of the student and so the exercises were as experientially based as was feasible without stretching the role-play beyond the limits of what was useful.

We began with an alliterative name game and then revised the differences between formal and informal learning and compared our conclusions with The Learning From Experience Trust (LET) materials (Handout 6). We were soon faced with the fundamental problem with experiential learning, which is how to know that learning has actually taken place. In other words, there is a difference between an experience and a learnt experience. 'I experienced a train ride this morning, but my thoughts were elsewhere.' What was the value of that experience? How do we turn an experience into a learnt experience? We used Kolb's cycle as an experiential exercise. This is a timed exercise and can be used as a problem-solving method or a reflective process to illustrate Kolb's theory. The students are asked to concentrate on an event or problem in their lives, either current or from the past. One minute is spent reflecting on those feelings. One minute is spent theorising or generalising from the reflections. Half a minute is spent making a decision or decisions and a further half-minute on determining future action. We compared the exercise with Kolb's theoretical cycle (see Chapter 1) and discussed the implications. (I am grateful to Brenda Rogers for introducing me to the timed exercise described above.)

We then returned to the work of our previous meeting and noted the main problem with unstructured learning – it lacks formal proof. The 'students' then worked through Handout 7 as a self-assessment exercise.

In the afternoon, we split into smaller groups to discuss what competences we thought admissions tutors would look for in prospective candidates. We then compared these with the competences elicited in a previous LET project and were much encouraged by the similarity of our conclusions (Handout 8). We concluded the day with a study skills exercise derived from a jig-saw reading I had used in facilitating women's studies classes, and then evaluated our progress thus far.

The difficulty in organising the training programme to meet the availabilities of the 'students' meant that we did not meet for another six weeks. We then held two further sessions.

Day 3: Day 3 was planned as an opportunity to explore and reflect on the process of MEC/APEL and its place within the ethos of the WEA. Our external moderator to the project – a Lecturer in Experiential Learning at Goldsmiths' College, University of London – gave us an overview of current practice in the field; and we assessed our own practice in relation to the 'four villages' (see Chapter 1).

Day 4: Day 4 was spent in examining the politics of APEL in relation to NVQs, in discussing our own future courses, and planning our programmes.

The training programme concluded with a group evaluation and I asked for individual assessments to be sent to me after a period of reflection.

Evaluation

(The following account is largely my own. There are few direct references to the tutors' evaluations. The reader is referred to Chapter 11 for a different approach to the 'collective' experience.)

The training programme was necessarily circumscribed by funding constraints and the time-scale of the project. Four days was hardly long enough to give tutors any more than an introduction to some of the processes and issues.

From the outset, I had wanted to explore the implications of facilitating experiential learning as relating to APEL practice. MEC courses, if they included the completion of portfolios for assessment, were included in this category.

Superficially, the project fell within 'village one' (assessing and accrediting prior experiential learning). This meant that many of the problems discussed earlier in this volume were going to be faced by the new team in their teaching. By immersing the tutors in the experiential process from the outset, I was hoping to accomplish two processes in one. Their experiences as students would alert them to the complexities of the process which their own students would undergo; their role as adult educators would inform their critique of the whole endeavour. Indeed, we found that the twin perspective created the environment for a rigorous assessment of each stage.

Obviously, the first problem was the sheer amount of material covered in Days 1 and 2. Although the tutors were acting as students, the work they covered in six hours would normally have taken as many weeks, and there would have been the reflective period between sessions. There was a danger that attempting too much would result in very little being absorbed, with the consequence that the tutors would feel even less prepared and more anxious than they had at the outset. But I took the risk, knowing from my own experience that it is only by working through one's first programme that one can begin to understand the complexities of the process.

I wanted the students to be aware of the available materials, but, more importantly, I wanted them to experience some of the contradictions in what they were trying to achieve so that they faced their group with a realistic assessment of future options and possibilities. Many students attend an MEC/APEL course thinking that it will change their lives. Sometimes it does – but our marginal position, with no formal outcomes, made it imperative that we all knew the limitations from the outset. As expected, this fact provoked the greatest anxiety and confusion. Most of the team placed themselves within 'village three' (interested in social change) or 'village four' (working towards individual development) yet placed the course within 'village one' (with the assumption of external assessment). The tensions expressed earlier in this book were reiterated by those who were especially critical of the functionalist/reductionist role that APEL might be demanding of them. Their criticism included the materials, which they felt to be culturally, gender – and to a large degree – class specific.

I noted in Chapter 1 that The Learning From Experience Trust exercises echoed Knowles' dictum that 'adults are what they have done'. The exercise designed to build individual confidence by asking students to review their experiences was successful up to a point. It did produce a mass of achievements of which the group could feel proud, but some noted their own inadequacy or competitiveness when looking at another's list. They were also critical of the stereotypical categories which, whilst eliciting 'achievements', also circumscribed them within the realms of the traditionally acceptable. The fact that 'Homemaking/Parenting' was the first category on the list, and therefore by implication perhaps more important than the following 'Paid Work', did not ease their irritation that the majority of adult students – i.e. women – were being patronised by their easy classification within the *status quo*. (I have to add, in fairness, that the LET materials were not intended to be used as a means of tutor training or as part of a group process. Yet, in terms of the concerns expressed in Chapters 1 and 2, I wonder about the consequences for the individual who wishes to pursue the MEC/APEL process as a sole activity.)

The second most important concern was how to clarify the distinction between education and counselling. My own experience had taught me that no MEC course should run without access to an independent counsellor. But then I might be accused of cowardice in trying to steer a course between dealing with the positive retrieval of skills and abilities and coping with the traumas of individuals' lives. The depth of pain that can often come to the surface requires more than the skills of a facilitator. On the other hand, by confronting our experiences and situating them within the broader context of women's lives in society, can we thereby offer individuals some comfort? Is this an appropriate role or objective? In terms of the MEC course, if facilitated within a gynagogic framework (see Chapter 2), it might also encourage collective action for social change.

The exercise involving the breakdown of the learning acquired in terms of skills and competences was also revealing in provoking resentment at the 'crudeness' of its classification. Yet the tutors' preference for looking instead at an accumulated sense of 'What I Learned' begged the question of what that learning actually entailed. Once again, we were faced with one of the crucial concerns of this book: how, and in what way, does learning impact upon the learner?

The paired exercises were considered particularly useful. Most of the tutors acknowledged that they had underestimated their achievements. Feedback and prompting from others gave them extra confidence to move on to 'own' what they had considered banal and not worth mentioning. If we bear in mind that this group consisted of educational 'successes' – with higher education backgrounds and demanding vocational commitments – then we have some idea of how much less likely the anxious 'returner' would be to 'own' her success. This gives pause for thought for those developing distance learning packages as a means of self-assessment because it illustrates how important or supportive the group can be in encouraging individual self-worth and in building confidence.

All of these issues were highlighted during Day 2. Many of the tutors felt extremely uncomfortable when asked to consider how they would deal with assessing experiential learning as a means of gaining entry to HE. They were aware that however significant experiences might be to the individual, they might not count as appropriate for entry. What damage could be done to less confident people, if, once again, they felt rejected or undervalued?

Their response to Kolb's cycle as an experiential exercise was also illuminating, given the concerns of this book. Some found it useful as a meditative technique and enjoyed the change of pace it represented, but all of them found it extremely difficult to compartmentalise their responses as the exercise required because 'it's difficult to separate thinking from feeling'.

Given the amount of work undertaken in the first half of the training programme, it was not surprising that the discussions in the ensuing two days would revolve around these issues and the broader politics of our endeavours. Some of the questions had been asked, some of the problems had been experienced but no one was under any illusion that the questions had been answered or the problems solved.

As one of the tutors wrote in her evaluation:

> *The exercises were useful to do and to record for future use as teachers – Good tools for empowering students but sensitivity and focus on the positive aspects of experience are crucial ... Realising the import and delicacy of the fact that the subject of APEL courses is someone's own LIFE up for scrutiny/evaluation (is) potentially, if not actually, nerve-racking; scary.*

CHAPTER FIVE

Making Experience Count at Ford Motor Company *

We regard this as one of the most exciting projects ever developed and one which benefits not only our employees but local communities where Ford has a presence.

John Hougham, speaking as Ford's Director of Personnel, is here describing the company's innovative Employee Development and Assistance Programme (EDAP). This had been established in agreement between the management and the trade union to provide learning opportunities 'for the purpose of personal development, advancement and progression'. It was one of the first schemes of its kind to operate in this country and was conceived as a means of promoting educational opportunity for the workforce. Each employee was entitled to a grant of up to £200 each year to attend a programme of liberal education. (Although some of the courses might lead to formal qualifications, the liberal/vocational divide was perceived in terms of EDAP's distinction from company-provided work-based training.) In 1993/4 the numbers of employees applying for the scheme had reached 87,000, which represented between 30 and 35% of the workforce. The range of courses included:

- languages
- computer studies
- craft skills – bricklaying, plastering, etc.
- GCSE and 'A'-levels; City and Guild certificates
- photography, music and all types of adult education
- basic skills, including maths, English and presentation skills

* Written with Elizabeth Draper
- Access to higher education courses.

The basic philosophy was outlined by Sandra Southee at a Return to Learn conference organised by the Kent Training and Enterprise Council. She argued that as a result of the programme 'everyone gains':

- employees develop their personal skills and knowledge
- the company benefits from the increase in employee loyalty generated by the gratitude felt for the new opportunities offered
- unions and local management have control of funds for the benefit of employees
- the company also benefits from a better educated and healthier workforce.

The programme was not restricted to the provision of courses. It had been apparent from the outset that if the scheme were to work, it would have to address the barriers to learning experienced by the potential participants. Not surprisingly, the problems found among employees at Ford have been indentified in many other educational arenas. They included:

- lack of time: family responsibilities; work schedules; shift work; unsocial hours
- cost: particularly among the less well-off
- attitudinal issues: no awareness of own learning needs; perceived lack of relevance of learning; no confidence to learn; stereotypes of education; fear of failure after 'failure' in school.

It is to the EDAP scheme's credit that these issues were taken seriously and a substantial investment was made to overcome the barriers. This response included:

- advice and guidance on available learning opportunities
- help in the selection of appropriate courses
- flexible provision of courses

- classes 'on site' before and after work
- widening access to educational opportunities
- workgroup classes – managers study with people from the shop floor
- grants of up to £200 to enable attendance on courses.

Our MEC course was not unique within Ford EDAP's provision. For example, Ray O'Connor, of Liverpool University, has a wealth of experience in the facilitation of portfolio preparation within the company. However, it was the first time that MEC had been offered at the particular plant in Essex with which we were working. The opportunity to place one of our six pilots within the EDAP scheme was provided as part of the collaborative link we enjoyed with Goldsmiths' College, which had pioneered much MEC/APEL development within the country in conjunction with The Learning From Experience Trust.

The analysis of the course which follows is less concerned with the already much-applauded acknowledgement, within an increasing number of companies, that by broadening learning outside the vocational domain, employees' work and commitment is usually enhanced. This chapter deals, rather, with questions which stem from the issues discussed in Section One. Notwithstanding the commitment shown by the Ford Motor Company to the educational needs, and problems, of a large number of its employees, the EDAP scheme is nonetheless operating within a particular cultural framework – a multi-national company geared to maximising productivity and profit. This course gave us the opportunity to examine the following particular issues:

- how can MEC be facilitated within a specific cultural climate, i.e. that of a multi-national company?
- what are the implications of concentrating on process within an organisation committed to outcomes and delivery?
- what are the implications regarding the transfer from the private and personal to the public arena: firstly with a group of colleagues who may be of higher or lower

levels within the employment hierarchy, and secondly within the broader domain of the company itself, with its distinct corporate image?

Taken at its simplest: what effect does the venue have on levels of disclosure?

(In the following accounts, the students' words are prefixed with an asterix to differentiate them from the tutor's.)

The MEC course at Ford EDAP was organised as a 20-hour programme, to run as a 10-week class of two hours per session. Six people enrolled on the course; five women and one man. They came from a variety of social and cultural backgrounds, one had a university degree, but they were all at middle-management level. They were employed as 'analysts', 'schedulers' or 'co-ordinators' in such departments as Sales, Human Resources (Personnel) and the EDAP programme itself.

Their reasons for joining the course were discussed at the beginning of the first session. They were largely expressed in vocationally-based and practical terms:

> * I wanted to do a degree course. A portfolio seemed to be the 'in' thing and I thought it would be good if I had one as well.

Yet even at the first session, as students became involved with the philosophy and practice of experiential learning, these 'presenting' reasons were gradually cast aside in a greater appreciation of their underlying and hitherto unconscious motives. They were asked to evaluate the first class and proffered the following comments. The session had:

> * stimulated the thinking process

> * (given) time for thought

> * (given) time for me

> * (encouraged) looking at things in a more diverse way

> * (laid down) no strict limits on areas for discussion.

These rather tentative comments reflected the underlying reasons for joining which continued to rise to the surface as the course progressed. The following assessment comes from the tutor's report:

> *It seems that most of them enrolled because they wanted to do something more with their lives, they wanted to think about change, they were suffering boredom and frustration with themselves and the established routines. There was a sense that they wanted to 'rock their boats' and push them out, somewhere, perhaps as yet unchartered ... This course brought them an ideal opportunity in which to take their first crucial step on their desired path for a new direction.*

However, these deeper reasons produced feelings of anxiety and insecurity. From the outset, there was a tension between the 'safety' of the presenting aims and intentions – couched in largely vocational terms – and the much more complex individual motives which were compounded with issues relating to self-awareness and self-image. It was a tension which was 'played out' in a number of ways throughout the programme; in a drama in which the company, and its organisational structures, played a key role.

As with all of the tutors on our team, Elizabeth's teaching practice is based upon facilitative methods which are aimed at encouraging trust, support and equality between the class members and in relation to the tutor:

> *The content of each session was varied, open-ended and flexible. The atmosphere I tried to generate ... was one of easy informality.*

Given the tension outlined above, it is hardly surprising that there was resistance to the informality that Elizabeth was trying to create. It 'flew in the face of the institution in which the course was based and the students' expectations'. The following comments are taken from the students' own assessments:

* *Initially I thought it was not geared enough to the working environment. We seemed to concentrate on out of work ambitions.*

* *I was not sure if it would serve my purpose.*

* *The worksheets were too informal – some were not even typed out ... that's not very professional.*

Elizabeth was convinced that these formal expectations were exacerbated by the timing of the course as well as by its location:

> *I often wondered if discussion and revelation were hampered by the fact that the course was conducted alongside work colleagues, within the place of work, and at 5pm immediately after work finished. All three factors ... cramped the style of the participants. It was hard to let go of work: work was why they were there in the first place, they'd just finished work, they were with work colleagues. It took a while to wrench them away from this strong mental frame, some could never really break out of it.*

She was also sensitive to the potential effects on the students of their immediate environment. The classroom, although comfortable and air-conditioned, had the same impersonality ' which is common to corporate buildings everywhere. There were no windows and no access to natural light:

> *This course deals with emotions, with people's inner lives and how they have negotiated with their outside lives: to be enclosed in such an inward-facing interior, I believe, places extra pressure on the whole experience ...*

It was possible, of course, that the tutor was merely projecting her own feelings on to the students, in seeking to explain the friction which was integral to the initial weeks of the course. It was an issue which was eventually addressed openly and

Elizabeth asked if the students would have felt differently had the course been held outside the work environment:

* Yes. I think attending in a Ford workplace made me hold back because I have a professional front to keep up and therefore my trusting of others was slow and didn't occur.

* Probably; I think there is the feeling that what you say may just be 'leaked' on the company grapevine.

The degree to which the initial reticence of the students was a result of the institutionalisation of the programme is a moot point. Surely there are a number of factors here which we have to take into account if we are to provide the safest environment in which our students may explore the value of their experiences. The only male student left after the first week. Two of the others attended only some of the sessions. It was later disclosed that the reasons were personal. Only two of the original five attended each session. The course was also disrupted because two Bank Holidays fell within the weeks of the programme.

Yet despite all of the problems, the dynamic within the group began to change. The initial reticence and suspicion gradually gave way to a greater trust that the process of the course could prove beneficial after all. Two exercises seemed to be of particular value in helping the process to coalesce. They were both concerned with reflecting on the external factors which have influenced one's life and the degree to which the more negative aspects might be changed. In other words, they encouraged the making of connections in an attempt to suggest that passivity in the face of apparently overwhelming circumstances might be overcome by a process of *active* re-appraisal. The 'ME' exercise has a strong visual element:

the student draws a picture, a series of (ideally multi-coloured) circles surrounding 'ME', which encapsulate the various influences orbiting around the self. Some you can visualise kicking away from you, creating a space for others to float freely nearer to you. This can be quite a liberating, *empowering exercise; it seemed to be with this particular group.*

Both exercises were mentioned in the students' final evaluations as having been particularly important. Yet what was interesting was less the *re*-appraisal element than the implication that there is never enough time for even initial appraisal to take place:

> *The 'ME' exercise was very revealing. The 'People I admire' also. I found it a wonderfully self-indulgent time, thinking about me, and what I wanted to do and having somebody (apparently) interested enough to listen (fellow students and tutor).*

The issue of time proved to be a recurring theme throughout the course. The final four sessions were re-scheduled to run for three rather than two hours. This was partly to 'catch up' with the sessions missed during the Bank Holidays, but it also arose from the students' complaint that the sessions were too short; that 'just as things were warming up and relaxing it was time to go.' The three-hour slot encouraged greater intimacy and helped to develop a measure of 'trust and good feeling'.

It was also apparent to both the tutor and the students that there was not enough time in the 20-hour programme to complete a portfolio exercise. As Elizabeth noted in her report:

> *Twenty hours is simply not long enough in which to identify portfolio objectives, find the evidence ... there would be specific journeys which would have to be undertaken: emotional/nostalgic as well as physical/practical. This group were still in the mental stage of bracing themselves to dig back for evidence when the course ended.*

However, given the original (as stated) reasons for joining the course, it was interesting to note that the 'failure' to complete a tangible piece of work which could have been shown to others was considered relatively unimportant by the end of the programme.

* I didn't do a written portfolio although I believe I have started a practical one.

* The main issue was that I must have time for myself and I must try and be myself. I'm not sure I can achieve this! But at least I have something to aim for.

This shift in perspective was obviously partly encouraged by the 'intimacy' created during the latter part of the course. Yet there was another side to the issue of intimacy which rendered it a potentially double-edged sword. Because attendance was erratic, there were sometimes too few students to maintain the very fine balance between willing disclosure and pressured 'confession'. Elizabeth notes again that:

generating a 'safe' environment was made more difficult because the group was so small: at times only three or two students. This made the session that much more pressurised and personal, isolating individuals simply because there were too few of us, ironic though this may sound.

The 'irony' was compounded by the fact that much of the intensely personal material was disclosed to the tutor outside the class contact hours.

She urges that there should always be a recruitment process for MEC courses which advises prospective students of the emotional nature of much of the work. She concludes that attendance is inadvisable for anyone 'who is suffering from an experience they have not yet come to terms with, or are in the process of coming to terms with'.

* I didn't stop attending because I wasn't interested. I find it difficult to look back into my life, in fact it hurts. I didn't realise before I came to the course how many of my emotions may be drawn out and talking to strangers in the group made me feel insecure. I came to the course hoping that I would complete the portfolio and be able to take a degree course. However, it made me realise that work and education are not the 'be all and end all' and that what I really need is life. The

course wasn't designed for the result I had but I am, and will be forever, grateful. My children are moving forward all the time, now I think it's my turn.

The students were asked what advice they would give to students about to embark on a similar MEC programme. The preceding comment and the following one from another illustrate Elizabeth's anxiety whilst highlighting, once again, the vexed question of the distinction, or otherwise, between the educative and the therapeutic process.

> * *Take time before you attend the course to reveal the darker sides of your past to yourself. Come to terms with them. Write them down and read them back. Also reflect on the good times, realise your own strengths and weaknesses. Take down the brick walls as much as possible so that you are strong mentally and emotionally to accept the outcome. Because, in my case, the outcome was worlds away from what I thought I wanted.*

Elizabeth kept a journal of her thoughts and feelings whilst facilitating this MEC course. Her reflections mirror the shifts in the group process and encompass both the negative and the positive fluctuations that the complexity of the course dynamic generated. What follows gives us some indication of the intellectual and ethical dilemmas which this kind of work lays bare.

> *I feel depressed. I'm finding this difficult.*
>
> *This course can conjure up the idea of magic solutions to past mistakes, but there are no solutions, and that's hard both for them and for me ... high hopes have to be brought down to earth ... It's hard for me bringing this 'whacky' course into the conventions of Ford ... help!*
>
> *Is it possible to 'fail' this course? Who judges and what are the criteria? How can you put people's experiences, and their reflections upon them, up for examination, to be scrutinised and graded? To fail someone, or downgrade them, has horrifying implications. Can I be involved with such a thing as that?*

I feel doubtful about all of this ... about the practical outcome, the value in real terms, beyond the personal, of the portfolio. Just how recognised is it by academic institutions, for example? EVIDENCE? More evidence is needed of the successes in this area.

I find this an exciting and pioneering area. I believe in it. I can see how empowering it can be. But there are issues which need careful attention, a lot of improvements/clarifications need to be made about both the process and its possible outcomes.

Elizabeth's reflections mirror the contradictions that the MEC process produces in our experience of facilitating the programmes. What conclusions are we to draw from this particular course, situated, as it was, within the Ford EDAP programme?

The question that we wished to address within this particular project was the degree to which the nature of the venue, the workplace, would impinge upon the aims and objectives of the course. It is obvious that the initial expectations of the students were largely informed by the mores of the culture in which they worked. The tensions that were provoked by the difference between the tutor's facilitative approach and the more traditional, and hierarchical, assumptions which the students brought to the course produced a space in which the implications could be explored. However, the project also taught us that the consequences of having such a space do not easily translate into a straightforward shift in personal perception, with the concomitant acknowledgement of new possibilities and different directions to pursue. There is a stage in-between. We cannot simply assume that a shift in focus will automatically lead to a fresh ownership of new-found skills and enhanced potential. The issue is not one of *re-appraisal* but of *appraisal*. The emphasis on 'looking anew' at one's life and the factors that have informed it can be liberating, but it can also produce the emotional minefield that is, perhaps more properly, the 'stuff' of psychotherapy. The distinction between the educative and the therapeutic is one of the central questions which the MEC process evokes. Perhaps the distinction is more apparent where the course is situated in an environment which is not particularly conducive to an analysis of the broader social factors which inform who and what we are. This is a point which will be elaborated when we come to compare this programme with those placed within different milieux.

> *Dealing with people's lives, the 'mistakes' they feel they have made and that they can learn from but not undo, is like working in an emotional minefield. Always bringing out the positive, as the facilitator, you are aware that you are but seconds away, at any given moment, from the 'flip-side'. And this has to be avoided where possible, which involves enormous energy on the part of the facilitator who is steering the group through 'it all'. An exhausting, challenging but enormously rewarding process.*

These are Elizabeth's conclusions. Despite the contradictions in her own account of the project, she feels that the project was, in the final analysis, worthwhile. One might be tempted to conclude that the programme was merely the initial stage of a journey which could have profound consequences and resonances beyond the confines of its stated remit. Perhaps the question which we have to address as educators is the degree to which we should be aware of, and take some responsibility for, the repercussions of the aftermath.

> ** I went on this course because I felt I needed a 'Project' and I couldn't decide whether to pursue something work-related or to do with other things. I have not really found the answer to these problems. However, the issues raised on this course were more fundamental to my life as a whole and I'm surprised and happy about that.*

CHAPTER SIX

Voices from the Margins: MEC as Outreach *

In a world where language and naming are power, silence is oppression, is violence (Adrienne Rich).

This chapter discusses two of our courses which fell within the broad category of outreach provision. These programmes were targeted at those members of our community who would not normally seek out adult education provision.

It is easy to make sweeping generalisations when talking about 'outreach'. Despite the well-intentioned efforts of outreach workers, ourselves included, the term very often serves as a mechanism for heightening 'difference' between sections of people rather than fostering understanding. We seek to support empowerment via an increased awareness of the *shared* nature of so many of our problems; but the students on these courses need desperately to be made aware of the value of their *uniqueness*. One of the key questions to consider, therefore, is how valid is the MEC/APEL process when used with groups who are marginalised from the societal privileges accorded adults who, more obviously, fit the prescription that 'adults are what they have done'.

The issue is cyclical in begging one of the fundamental tenets underpinning work with the 'disadvantaged'. What does the word 'empowerment' actually mean? Is it a question of trying to encourage feelings of greater self-worth or should it attempt to encompass a social critique in the hope of fostering collective action and change? In other words, how do we articu-

* *Written with Sue Forward and Greg Crowhurst*

late the relationship between self-identity and the societal factors which inform who and what we are?

The first section describes a project run in conjunction with
Social Services. The tutor for this course was particularly concerned with the problem of speaking 'on behalf' of the women
on the programme. What follows is our collective attempt at
providing a space for their reflections whilst protecting their
anonymity and respecting the factors which had brought them
to the programme.

The second section describes the work undertaken in facilitating a group of students with 'special needs'. This project was
even more concerned with the problems relating to self-identity. Most of the students had lost their sense of connectedness
to others. To what extent could they 'make sense' of their experiences if they could not relate them to a broader arena?

Women at the Margins

*I have found myself unable to write adequately about this
course for three reasons. Firstly, I am at present a full-time
undergraduate, struggling to maintain my own identity and
suffering from pressure of work. Second, facilitating the
APEL programme brought out fully for me my own
frustrations about the lack of opportunities and the waste of
talent and ability we endure in this country and I am still
dealing with these tensions within myself. Third, and most
importantly, I feel I cannot accurately represent other
women's experiences. If outcomes were that easily monitored
APEL would not be the ambiguous programme which it is.
Only the participants can know what they gained from the
course – that is true learner-managed learning.*

[Despite these anxieties, Sue, the tutor on this course, provided
an account of the structure of the programme and it is her
words that follow.]

The APEL project in South Kent began as an outreach enterprise initiated by a voluntary member of the local WEA branch.

This initiative was taken up by the WEA South Eastern District under the APEL umbrella. The course was recruited via the social workers' and health visitors' network. This was achieved by word of mouth and a flyer targeted at relevant sections of the social service network. Social services provided the accommodation (at one of their centres), transport and creche facilities. The course ran for 10 weekly sessions of two hours each. The initial recruitment was of 10 women, ranging in age from 18 to 52. All had left school at the first opportunity, a few felt they had 'learning difficulties', one had some vocational qualifications. After four weeks of fluctuating attendance the group reduced to a committed core of five women.

Course Aims

The aims of the course were to provide an opportunity for unwaged and/or single mothers to:

- gain in confidence, self-esteem and self-responsibility
- learn to work together as a group whilst respecting individual needs and differences
- reflect on past experiences and recognise strengths and skills gained
- identify areas where there was a desire to gain new skills and knowledge
- explore ways in which acquired skills could be used in new ways or situations
- investigate opportunities for gaining new skills and knowledge.

Course Methods

We used ourselves in small group work and whole group discussions. We role-played, brainstormed, used flip-charts, expressed ourselves in art, drank a lot of coffee, laughed and cried. The students took time, outside the sessions, to gather information and investigate opportunities. In the latter half of the course, we used materials adapted from The Learning From Experience Trust and the WEA *Getting Started* pack. In addition, the group also used exercises from *Build Your Own Rainbow*

(Hopson and Scally, 1991), as an aid to exploring possible future directions.

The First Session

Why are they here – what do they expect – what do they want? We spent the first half of the first session on gentle 'getting to know us' exercises. Then we moved on to explore, in groups of three, what they expected and what they wanted from the course. It was the discussion which followed the small groups session which set the agenda for the rest of the course.

Five of the women felt they had been 'sent' to the course by social workers or health visitors; one was very resentful of this fact, the other four were resigned to it 'as a way of life'. The other participants all felt they had made the choice to attend, although based on inadequate information as to what to expect. Drawing on their own thinking and what they had previously been told, they said they *expected*:

- to be taught how to do things better
- to have to learn to use a computer
- perhaps to learn to do wallpapering or something like that.

What they said they *wanted* was:

- a chance to socialise
- a couple of hours without the kids
- to feel confident
- to be able to say what I mean.

One woman (the only one in paid employment) said she was a Nursing Auxiliary and had 'been NVQ'd'; she wanted to find out more about NVQs with a view to becoming an assessor. This opened up the whole debate about APEL and accrediting transferable skills. After briefly describing NVQs and APEL, I sat back and listened. They all seemed instantly to recognise the possible value of identifying and accrediting skills, the potential for opening up employment and education opportunities for those without traditional qualifications, although most felt it had little to offer them, or that they did not have much to offer. However, one women was able to sum up the dilemma for us all when she said:

> *APEL could be used to keep people in their places, in low-skilled, low-paid work. And what does it matter anyway, when there aren't enough jobs to go round? Anyway, I can't afford to work, I'd lose my benefits and have to pay for childcare, we'd be even worse off than we are now. I would like to go out to work, I really miss it, but looking after my kids is important too.*

My own preconceived ideas for the course 'went out of the window' from that moment on. Although I kept the idea of an APEL portfolio constantly in mind, I found myself reacting to the participants' agenda and revising the course from week to week; sometimes half-way through a session. What happened from then on and what the students gained from the experience, only they can tell you.

At this point, Sue's narrative ceases. In our discussions regarding the feasibility of including her course within this volume, it was decided that such inclusion would only be warranted if the students could furnish their own stories. The question was whether it was appropriate to seek out the group members and invite them to contribute and formulate a framework within which their contributions could be heard whilst, at the same time, protecting their privacy.

I contacted our colleague at Social Services. She was willing to approach the women on my behalf and they invited me to meet them in one of their homes. What follows is their account of the process of the course. It was compiled over several meetings and after we had explored the most effective ways of gathering their words together. We tried tape-recording a general discussion about the effects of the programme but this proved difficult to manage because the women were inhibited by the 'machine' and complained that it stopped the flow of their talk.

They were excited by the project because it gave them the opportunity to 'share with other women like ourselves the possibilities that *may* actually be open to them'. They wanted it to be 'real' and so asked that their first names be included in any published account. Together, we decided upon a set of questions and some of them offered to write their own accounts. Two of the women were less confident of their written skills and so a third suggested she acted as recorder.

These are the questions which formed the basis for our discussions:

1. What did you think the course was trying to achieve? What were its aims?
2. Would you say it was successful or not?
3. Can you give me some examples?
4. What did you in particular gain from the course?
5. What are your plans for the group now?
6. What did you learn about your skills and what do you want to learn in the future?

The first responses are those from the group as a whole. They are recorded here in the order in which they were articulated. They are followed by fuller accounts as offered by two of the women. (With thanks to Alison, Angie, Julie, Marie and Micki, and to Ruth Ross and Rita Bell for their support.)

Confidence, self-awareness. It gave us time to talk freely without the children.

At first it seemed more like a discussion group than a course, we think that may be why so many dropped out, it wasn't till later that we did any worksheets; for us it was successful.

Confidence, got me out of the house to meet people, taught me something about myself, freedom to talk without worrying about it going any further.

Confidence, meeting people, getting rid of (child's name) for a while as I was in a bed-sit for most of the course, seeing a different set of walls, meeting female friends. Also it gave (child's name) a chance to play with other children as she is an only child.

Got me out of the house, meeting other people and eventually talking to other people, got us thinking about ourselves and what we could achieve, using our brains again when it came to the worksheets. During the break we went into the kitchen and could talk, smoke and generally relax.

Confidence, learning to look at things from other people's point of view. I stopped worrying about minor issues and therefore I became happier within myself. I stopped hiding behind a false front.

Looking at our interests on the worksheets I wasn't surprised at the first results as I knew I liked practical (things), which was my top group. The second group surprised me, which was 'social and administration' which were areas I wouldn't have thought of entering. I've already done a two-year year chef's course at college so I wouldn't go back again, but I intend to do some form of catering when my children are at school.

I didn't complete all of the worksheets but I would like to go on to adult education as I have a problem with English and maths, and I would like to be able to help my children.

I found out that I have a brain. I am looking for a course at the moment. I am interested in archaeology, photography, ancient history.

The results from the (interests) worksheets were very accurate. The first result was 'social' which includes nursing and medicine, both are great interests of mine. Then came 'investigative'. I like finding things out. The last group was 'artistic'. I enjoy making things. I would like to go back to college to do GCSEs in English and I would like to do a business studies course so that I could run my own art and craft shop.

Understanding myself and others

The course has given me the opportunity to find myself, knowing the person I really want to be and the position I want to aim for. During the weeks I have attended, different and very interesting issues have been raised, and so it has opened my eyes very wide, seeing things in a different light whereas beforehand I was so negative.

People at this course have been so helpful and understanding, including my tutor, whom I must thank very much.

It's funny. You look at yourself and think you are the only person in the world with all these problems. Then you listen to others and yours are minor ones. Considering everything, I am lucky in a lot of ways, but never stopped to think about it as I was so wound up with myself.

I am actually trying to understand myself now in more ways than one and actually believe there is a lot more to life. But you have to go for it yourself and make it happen. As someone said to me a long time ago: think positive and positive things will happen. I guess I must have forgotten!

I have had a long period where I have relapsed, but thanks to you all I can actually see it's about time I made a comeback. Now I have taken it one step further as I am enrolling for a 20-week course in counselling starting in September. Without the help of you all and the patience of my tutor I could not have done this.

Thank you all.

Meeting the unexpected

My health visitor popped in one day and announced, 'There's a course starting called Making Experience Count'. 'What's it about?' I asked. 'I'm not sure but I think you'll like it.' Reluctantly, I said I would give it a go.

Still not knowing what I was letting myself in for I went along with my friend. I couldn't help wondering from the vague leaflet that I'd been given if I was going to be on an 'Improvers' course for home maintenance or if I would be expected to become a computer wizard overnight. When we got there, Sue introduced herself. She was totally different to what I'd expected. She was really friendly and did her best to put us at ease. I think I'd expected someone who was completely flawless and perfect, an android instead of a human. I was surprised to find a couple of mature ladies on the course but it really helped having their points of view ... The first part of each meeting was set out so that we had an informal chat about how we were coping with any problems that we had, the second half was self-analysis time and what a shock that was. When I started I was basically against men after a break-up in a relationship that left me devastated. I decided that anything a man could do, I would do better, I decided I could have more fun being unattached. I can see that it was all a mask, my way of coping with life. As the course progressed I found real confidence and gradually I lost the mask. I was admitting more to myself; instead of hiding facts I would face them. Five of us decided to carry on meeting ... to find a way of sharing our experiences with other women and help them to overcome feelings of being trapped and isolated.

My life has definitely changed over the past year and for the better. I feel happier with myself now, where I used to worry about minor issues like 'God, I'm overweight, I've got to lose weight'. Now I'm happier to be a bit overweight I have fun. I actually like myself now which I didn't before. Now I've stopped worrying about my weight I find I lose weight without trying, even when I don't want to.

Issues of Educational Responsibility

Before commenting on the preceding account it might be useful to describe what has happened to the women's group since the course finished. The last speaker mentioned that it was their intention to find some way of sharing their experiences with other women. It was also our intention, as facilitators of an outreach programme, to try and allocate resources to enable this specific project to continue.

One of the problems facing workers in this field is the difficulty of maintaining support when the intial seedcorn funding has ceased. This fact is only one of those which differentiates outreach work from mainstream adult education. Liberal adult education programmes, whether undertaken via the local authority, university continuing education departments or the WEA, are part-funded by the fees that the students pay. Most outreach provision has to be free to the students for the simple reason that they could not afford to pay, even if they regarded the 'purchase' of a course as something worth extracting from the family budget. There are some monies available from a variety of sources with which to initiate programmes, but it is extremely difficult to secure further funds with which to extend the 'pilots'.

This fact, in turn, leads to the broader issue of educational responsibility. We are all familiar with the 'barriers to learning' experienced by those who have gained least from our educational system. They have been well-documented and need no repetition here. But for those of us who work within this field, the assumption that the one-off programme will lead to integration in the educational mainstream is patently absurd. Most of these students find themselves at the margins of our political and economic spheres of influence. It takes time to establish a forum in which these hitherto silenced voices may come to believe that they will be heard. And this is only the first step. The ethic of 'difference' upon which our society is predicated is hardly susceptible to a relative whisper from the outer edges. To reiterate it succinctly: 'And what does it matter anyway, when there aren't enough jobs to go round?' So what is the role of the 'educator'? Providing a 'space' is the first necessity; but it is surely irresponsible to then abandon the project when that 'space' is beginning to be viewed as a site for exploration and development.

In this event, we were able to use some of our District's dwindling resources, which had been put aside for 'disadvantaged' work, to fund a further programme for the same group of women and others who would be recruited anew via Social Services. This course, facilitated by another member of the MEC team, led, in turn, to the establishment of a 'Women and Health' project which was funded by the local Health Promotion Unit (HPU). The programme of courses is still running. Our colleagues at the social services centre want the work to continue and will probably share the costs of yet another programme with the HPU in the coming year.

Of the original core group of five women, three are still attending and one of them has been employed by Social Services as assistant to the tutor. None of them has begun the courses which they said they wished to pursue. The second course comprised eight regular attenders, whilst the third, and current programme, attracted 12, with others now waiting to join. This has led to another problem which is related to our discussion. I have already stated that this kind of work requires a long-term commitment on the part of the educational providers. We may have secured funding for *one* more programme. Are we to begin anew with those waiting in the wings or are we to keep that space for another continuation course? Our colleagues at Social Services are concerned that some of the 'more confident' women should now be moving into mainstream education or the world of work. Indeed, one of the students has now completed an Access programme and is also working for a local volunteer bureau. Another found a full-time job and a third is working on a part-time basis. But the others have declared themselves unready to leave the group. They want the opportunity to study at a more rigorous level and have identified 'Women in History' as a topic, but they feel they need the security of the group, and their current tutor, if they are to embark upon a more academic endeavour. They have also, at the most basic level, expressed their 'need' to remain together whatever programme they pursue.

The ideal solution would be to generate sufficient funds to allow for two programmes to run in the forthcoming year. As a compromise, it has been suggested that the student who has been paid an assistant's fee might be willing to run a course for those on the waiting list, whilst the WEA tutor maintains the existing course. The obvious problem with this is the issue of exploitation. Why should the student not be paid the full amount if she is undertaking the same degree of responsibility as our regular tutor? But we do not have the funds to pay both.

There is another, and related, problem which is well-known to facilitators of outreach work. The underlying principle upon which all work of this kind is based is that the facilitator functions in precisely that mode. Her responsibility is to encourage the students to utilise the space they have been given to articulate *their own* needs, and thence to re-claim it for their own purposes. Yet the danger lies in crossing the very fine line between facilitation and fostering a culture of dependency. Have the women become too reliant upon the group and the tutor in terms of expressing their increasing confidence and feelings of self-worth? I argued in Chapter 2 that the journey towards autonomy is more problematic for a woman because she is still socially constructed largely in relation to others. We should therefore not be surprised that the women have declared their need for each other. But what should be the consequence of this? Should we perhaps not be celebrating the fact that the group has generated its own culture of mutual support and growth, which, if translated towards the wider community, could engender projects for collective action and change?

This issue of individual or collective process brings us back to one of the questions posed at the beginning of this section: what value did the MEC/APEL process have for these women?

Sue talked about her own ambivalence regarding the project. It was obvious from the outset that these women were highly unlikely to produce a finished portfolio. Their experiences would therefore not be translated into the public arena in a form which might lead to enhanced opportunity. Indeed, Sue changed the elements of the process in direct response to the needs of the women. Although both she and the tutor who followed utilised some of the worksheets and profiles from the

MEC project, the course could more broadly, and appropriately, be termed an assertiveness class or a self-advocacy programme or any one of the myriad labels that we use to give educational validity and acceptibility to the basic, and very simple, requirement for *space and time.*

These women's experiences have not been couched in the medium required for vocational or educational progression, but they have been 'counted' in their relations with each other and their individual reflections upon those relationships. It is to the disadvantage of us all that there are resources for such 'progression' (however unrealistic a concept that is) but not for the process.

Make Your Experience Count in Relation to 'Special Needs'

Greg was the only member of our MEC team who had facilitated work of this kind before the project began. He had been invited to join us because of his work with people with learning difficulties, and because he had facilitated MEC at Goldsmiths' College:

> *My purpose in doing this is to explore the potential of this approach within a mixed group and to learn how to facilitate this, to take into account all experiences and expectations.*

Together with colleagues, he had developed a Learning Manual (de Ville *et al.*, 1991) as an aid to organising experiences and formulating an Action Plan. He wished to establish whether the structure offered by the Manual would be of use to a group of learners who differed from the students who attended Goldsmiths' programmes. He described the recruitment process for his course in his report:

> *The course was advertised throughout [town's name] Community Living Service (for people with a learning difficulty) and through the [town's name] Forum (a mental health service user advocacy forum). The group comprised:*

- *one college lecturer*
- *three mental health service users*
- *two learning difficulty service users*
- *one support worker.*

There was one woman. There was no representation from the Black or Asian communities.

It was intended that the course would take the following 'route' in accordance with the Goldsmiths' model:

- Weeks 1– 4: Reflection upon participants' past experience
- Week 5: Tutorial and self-assessment
- Week 6: Looking at transferable skills
- Week 7: Reflection upon present learning experience
- Weeks 8 –10: Objectives and action planning and evaluation.

The first session was concerned with eliciting the students' expectations of the programme and what follows are some of their responses to the question 'what do you want to achieve from this course?':

To improve my self-regard and ability. To pass on to others.

To go out, get a meaningful relationship.

Whatever comes first.

The students were willing to disclose information about the 'life experiences' which had contributed to their inclusion in this particular course:

Special school, hospital, 'solitary imprisonment'.

Breakdown, 'A'-levels, engagement last month.

I can't remember much of my childhood. My teens lasted until I was 35 and then life became utterly dreadful ... I have learned many new things in the past few years ... usually succeed at what I do and then lose it.

I was sexually abused and then given 32 different medical labels.

It was apparent that the course was viewed by some in relation to a feeling that their lives were about to change. They were asked 'what stage of your life do you feel you are at?' Their responses included:

- crossroads
- the beginning of the rest of it
- a terminus
- start of a good part.

Two students left the course in the early stages. The only woman did not return after Week 2; another left because he had difficulty 'making sense' of the exercises. Greg noted in his report that he had 'often wondered, since, if the impact of filling in even more forms was simply too much for someone whose life is full of DSS forms.'

It was also becoming obvious to him that the way he had structured previous courses at Goldsmiths' begged too many questions about what students attending a college course expected in the way of educational delivery:

There was a difficulty about material and how to frame things. Maybe people could not relate to the way some information was presented ... I was apprehensive about how to approach this. Still feeling my way. I have a feeling that it will require more structure than past courses – maybe I will not be able to rely upon free-flowing discussion owing to lack of experience and (the) limited verbal skills of some of the participants ... I (have) to think carefully about my use of language ... The challenge was to choose as unobtrusive a structure as possible while still maintaining a clear focus and sense of direction ... To achieve this, I (have) used a mixture of: Direct Questioning; Presentations: Simple Activities (e.g. draw a triangle and mark 'where you're at').

The adaptations to the Goldsmiths' model began to take effect. Greg had noted that his earlier experiences with MEC had taught him that it usually took about three weeks for the meaning of the course to become apparent to the students: 'At this stage people realise that it's unlike any course they've been on. *They* are the course, their shared experience is the agenda.'

As the students began to internalise the dynamics of the programme:

the sessions developed, naturally, their own specific and almost 'peculiar' structure. The first half, up until coffee, was held in a discussion room. The second half was held sitting on settees, in the coffee lounge. It was during this second part that the group had its most intense and deep discussions. This presented its own challenges, as a facilitator. I was aware that I was leading the discussion, in as much as I was setting the agenda and the group looked to me to do this ... The sessions did, however, follow the same 'route'. The focus was always upon Action Planning following a reflection upon participants' life experience and situation.

One of the key issues that the course had to address was the initial failure to foster a group dynamic. This also marked its difference from previous courses that Greg had facilitated:

The group did not relate as a group in the beginning (maybe because of the damage individuals have suffered), instead people tended, it seemed, to be caught in a focus upon themselves rather than being aware of the connectedness of their experience ... There was, I felt, a hesitancy and a resistance to change – this is understandably 'scary'. This did result in 'game-playing' and avoidance, I felt, especially at the start of sessions.

Greg listed the 'learning blocks' he encountered on this particular programme:

- fear of failure
- being rejected
- sabotage
- lack of confidence.

An issue with participants was 'letting go' of the past, of the way they had learned to view themselves, others and the system. It can be safe, paradoxically, to say 'I cannot do anything about this'.

It is hardly surprising that questions such as these prompted the tutor to reflect upon the relationship between education and therapy:

The question has to be asked: Was it simply another form of group therapy? Or was it just about confidence building? I think that it included those two elements, to a certain extent. However, the course did not aim to provide therapy or confidence-building as such. The course aimed to enable people to reflect upon their past experience and to plan for the future, within a framework of self-empowerment.

Whether the aim of the course included confidence- building or not, the students' evaluations at the end of the programme clearly indicated that this had been a major element in how they perceived the value of the course.

In answer to the question: 'How has this course helped you identify your aims and objectives?' participants replied:

The course made me think about my life now, and I want to change it. I would like to be more independent. I have now applied to 'People to People' (for more independent living) and have had my first interview.

By clearing the undergrowth, demonstrating the effectiveness of my techniques, beliefs.

It has focused jumbled/scrambled elements into a clear tunnel. It has helped me understand that my fears were common in the group, just as different situations and that there is no harm in trying (what's to be scared of, only failure!).

It has helped me to like myself.

Greg added a note about one of the students:

With the man who was using learning difficulty services and who had very limited verbal communication skills, it is hard to judge how successful the course has been. His support worker wrote on his behalf: 'Sometimes, I found it hard to join in because I didn't understand the questions, etc.' This person, however, did choose, every Saturday, to get up early and come along ... Participants in the group came to speak more and more to him, and some challenged the support worker's sometimes dominant involvement.

I would like to concentrate upon two issues arising from this account. The first concerns the relationship between therapy and education. The second is related to the nature of the particular problems that the students on this course encountered in terms of their identification with the situations of other group members. In other words, the 'failure' of the students to foster a group dynamic at the outset forced the tutor to review the dynamics which he had depended upon in facilitating other MEC programmes.

The question of the relationship between 'education' and 'therapy' has recurred time and again in the accounts of the courses which we ran. It is an issue which will also be discussed in the following chapter and it evokes responses which, themselves, are predicated upon the particular 'belief systems' of the practitioners who are engaged with facilitating the process. During the training programme, we had discussed the particular problems inherent in facilitating a course in which the subject matter of both the discipline and the agenda is the students themselves. Some adult educationalists may argue that, whatever the subject under discussion, the identities of the students are inextricably involved in the learning that takes place. This claim is, indeed, central to women's education and two of the course team elucidate their response to the issue in the following chapter.

Whilst I would not disagree with this as a basic principle, I felt that the potentially explosive nature of the material on a Making Experience Count programme required the services of a counsellor who may be called upon should any individual find herself dealing with emotional resonances which could not be contained within the hours of class contact. I also urged the team to eschew the 'lifeline' approach and concentrate upon 'safer' topics to pursue. I have already acknowledged the naivety of this advice, but how else are we to deal with MEC as an educational process which confronts the constructions of our selves and our relation to the world?

This issue leads, in turn, to the value, or otherwise, of the group dynamic. Greg's course highlighted the problems that ensue when individuals are faced with sharing their anxieties with others. Although it was a basic tenet of our approach that we are constructed in relation to others, that fact can sometimes be of little consolation to those of us who have suffered damage at the hands of others. Trust is the key component of any successful group encounter. Yet how do we foster trust among individuals who are trapped in a cycle of insecurity and alienation?

It is to the credit of the participants on Greg's programme that their final evaluations spoke of increased self-confidence and enhanced self-worth. Unfortunately, we have no record of their progress after the course finished. One can only hope that the struggle to forge a group dynamic sustained the students after they had left the programme.

CHAPTER SEVEN

Making Experience Count With Women *

When women open the doors of their own lives and survey the carnage there in those out-of-the-way places, they most often find they have been allowing assassination of their most crucial dreams, goals, and hopes (Women Who Run With the Wolves, *Clarissa Pinkola Estes, 1992*).

This particular course gave us the opportunity to explore some of the issues raised in Chapter 2. They have been encapsulated in the following questions:

- to what extent does the MEC/APEL process differ when it is facilitated within a 'women only' or a mixed group?
- are there differences, predicated on gender, regarding the reclamation of prior experiential learning?
- to what extent can we differentiate between MEC/APEL and assertiveness training or consciousness-raising in the claim that 'this course has given me confidence and changed my life'?

Both of the tutors who facilitated this programme were members of the Brighton Women's Education Branch of the WEA South Eastern District. This had been established in 1987 in response to what was perceived as the specific educational needs of women in the Brighton area. It had enjoyed considerable success in providing a range of courses which included assertiveness, feminist filmand literary theory, art, lesbian issues and culture, history, etc.

* Written with Sara Bragg and Chris Pegg

The Women's Branch was itself an extension of the WEA's commitment, from its inception, to the educational needs of women:

> *If the WEA is to gain any substantial victory in its campaign against ignorance and injustice, men and women must be fighting side by side. Their cause, their interests are inseparably bound together. Neither party can march by itself without endangering both its own safety, and that of the party it has left, and if one ceases to make progress, the other is held back too; so, of all the special efforts the WEA has to make today, perhaps none is more important than the special effort it is making on behalf of women (Ida Hony, Secretary of the Women's Department, WEA, 1912).*

In the political climate of the 1990s, Hony's words might be misconstrued as arguing against a space for 'women-only' provision. However, her comments did not stem from the easy, and misguided, assumption that 'women have won the war for equality and no longer need to be separate in order to explore their place in the world'. Indeed, she stated in words which have no less relevance today that women 'are far readier to give an opinion or take part in a discussion when the committee or class is composed entirely of members of their own sex.'

In 1989, the WEA published a Policy Statement outlining the ethos as well as the aims and objectives of women's education:

> *Women's education aims to empower women in their own lives and within society and to challenge structural inequalities. It roots itself in conceptions of change rather than notions of disadvantage ... Women's education is not a subject but an interdisciplinary, cross-curriculum approach and perspective. (It) challenges the 'one-sidedness' of our knowledge, by putting women into the curriculum and by identifying and remedying the sexist bias of traditional subjects like history, psychology, law and literature. In doing so it acts as a challenge to the complacencies of the mainstream. Equally, by concentrating on dissolving the*

unreal boundaries which exist between fields of subject expertise and between thinking and feeling it also has this effect (WEA, 1989).

No one can deny that the ethical and methodological sweep of women's education has had a telling effect upon our mainstream educational system during the past 15 years. We have seen changes to the school curriculum based upon studies of socially constructed gender biases within learning styles. We have seen the plethora of women's studies programmes at undergraduate and postgraduate level within higher education. We have also witnessed a publishing explosion in the number of texts written specifically for a feminist market.

Yet only five years after the WEA Policy Statement we are also witnessing the effects of an anti-feminist backlash which is threatening women-only spaces and declaring that 'equal opportunities has gone too far'.

Chapter 2 deals in depth with the issues raised here. I would only wish to point out a further political and methodological principle which informed the tutors' (Sara and Chris) work and, therefore, our current discussion. The words are, once again, taken from the WEA Policy Statement:

A central place is given in all women's education to recognising and valuing the life experience of the students which has often in the past been viewed as secondary to the learning of more abstract knowledge. Both course content and process are based on the assumption that the personal is the political. While the experience of the student is obviously one of individual development and personal growth, the collective experience and aspirations of women are also a central theme. To be effective women's education must be rooted in and shaped by women's lived experience – historical and current, personal and collective. In working to engage the full capacities of all students it seeks to combine clarity and excitement of thought and theory with attention to feelings, circumstances and the boundaries which circumvent women's lives.

How relevant these words, particularly the last sentence, are to the lived experience of facilitating Making Experience Count it is the purpose of this chapter to investigate.

The following account is taken from the tutors' report. Apart from a few minor changes to their text for the sake of brevity, I have chosen to rely almost entirely upon their own words because their analysis reflects the concerns and illustrates the questions posed at the beginning of this chapter. For a fuller theoretical perspective, the reader is once again referred to Chapter 2.

Background Information and Course Aims

The course was held at the Brighton Unemployed Centre, which had originally been set up by the WEA and the Trades Union Council. Not only was there a historical link enabling co-operation, and obviously an appropriate ethos for the course, but also the only free daily creche in Brighton was based there. Because some of our students were users of the Centre, they were already familiar with the creche workers and knew the standards of care that were provided.

The programme was originally planned as a 10-week course in sessions of two hours each. It later became necessary to extend it by three weeks; even so, some students had still not been able to complete their portfolios by the end. Extra funding from another source, the Centre for Continuing Education at Sussex University, was eventually obtained for some more portfolio development classes, but by the time we had managed to set them up the impetus had perhaps been lost and attendance was poor. In the end, therefore, the course consisted of 13 sessions; four looking at past experiences and reflecting on them, and a session in the form of a presentation from the local Careers Advisory Service. Then followed six weeks' work on portfolio development, one session on an interview simulation exercise, and an evaluation.

In drawing up the course aims we tried to make the language accessible to our prospective students. However, in evaluation, some students did comment that we could have expressed these aims still more simply and that it took a while to understand how they were going to be met.

The course aims as we originally conceived them were as follows:

- to identify what you have done in your life, including the skills used in everyday living, and what you've learnt from them
- to recognise what you've achieved, to improve confidence and to consider your strengths
- to identify general abilities ('competences') based on skills and knowledge learnt through experience that can be applied in other situations
- to develop plans for future directions in life, work or education
- to develop a portfolio with evidence of your achievements
- to increase your knowledge of the opportunities available to you.

These aims were written on paper, prominently displayed in every session and referred to throughout the course. We also wrote up the objectives of each individual session and began each session by clarifying them. The salient points from some of our group discussions were also displayed. By the end of the programme, the walls of our room were covered with the visible evidence of the group's work.

Our general pedagogic method was that students spent some time on their own reflecting on an experience, question or issue which had been set by us, then talked to a partner about it. We asked participants not to talk to the same person all the time, although some particular preferences and friendships inevitably arose. The students then shared with the whole group. We found that this structure did create a supportive and open group atmosphere, although, initially, the students found this process both exposing and difficult. Our teaching strategy also tried to take into account the possibility that some students might lack confidence about writing and spelling.

Most of the students had seen the leaflet in the library, some had been students on other courses run by ourselves and had been contacted directly. Sixteen women attended the first session, undoubtedly encouraged to do so by the fact that the course was free. However, there were many more than had been expected, and so with two tutors and a community worker observer, the small room was cramped and crowded. Some women later commented on how 'panic stricken' and intimidated they were by being confronted with such a large group. One suggested that the 'drop-out' rate might have been lower if the initial sessions had not been so overwhelming.

During the introductions it became clear that most students had no definite aims in mind or clear expectations about the course; the prevailing motivation was curiosity and a desire to increase their confidence and find out about other opportunities available to them.

Out of the initial 16 students, two did not return after the first two sessions; we assume that they simply decided that the course was not appropriate for them. Three left during the first half of the course, two had found work and one left for further study. One student (whose attendance was disrupted by the illness of her children) dropped out, but notified us that she would like to do the course at a later stage. One left due to ill-health. Another left at the end of the first half because she already knew which direction she was pursuing (a teacher training course, on which she had a place for the autumn) and felt that she did not need to complete a portfolio.

Eight remained with the course until the end. They were aged between their early thirties and their late forties. Some were in part-time paid employment, some unemployed and one was self-employed. Five were parents, all with children under 10. One student was British Asian, there were two Irish women, the rest were white British, including one Scottish woman. One was a graduate (who nevertheless felt that she had failed to build upon her qualifications), two were considering going on to higher education, and the rest were concerned with improving their basic educational skills or employment prospects.

Course Outline

The course used much of the material available from The Learning From Experience Trust (LET), albeit in modified form where we felt it necessary. While we have briefly referenced the material, we have focused our account around the processes of developing and teaching the course and the issues that arose during it.

In the first session, after introductions and discussion of the differences between 'formal' and 'informal' learning, the students began to complete the 'Reviewing Your Experience' exercise (Handout 1). Some of these experiences were listed on flip-chart paper, ostensibly to celebrate the group's collective skills. However, it was noticeable at this early stage that some students were reticent about naming their experience and lacked confidence in their skills. One student, who had established and run several design and dressmaking companies, listed all her dressmaking skills under the category of 'domestic skills'.

The second session began with a paired discussion about how the students felt about taking part in the programme. The women were given an opportunity to express their doubts, difficulties and uncertainties about the course and we tried to deal with them. They were then asked to write down individually what they had had to organise in order to get to the session. The results were collated by us and used in subsequent sessions. This exercise provided a simple and effective way of recognising the multitude of often overlooked abilities that women utilise in managing and co-ordinating not only their own lives but those of their partners and children.

We then continued reviewing experiences and introduced the concept of general competences using as example *A Family Experience* (Handout 4). The students were then asked to begin analysing one of their own experiences in the same way in order to elicit the competences involved. This proved to be a difficult task. The concept of 'competences' was unclear to many of them. A more serious problem was that many women found themselves unable to focus on anything but negative experiences, as became evident from the atmosphere in the group, and as they explained in the evaluation at the end of the session. At that stage, all we were able to do in response was to promise to focus on these feelings at the start of the next session. We spent time after the class with one student who was particularly distressed.

During the subsequent week, we met to try and analyse the different types of fear and negativity that the women seemed to be experiencing. We identified three main problems:

- painful personal experiences that women had undergone recently – such as loss and grief – and the fears surrounding these
- focusing exclusively on negative experiences in the past, i.e. those which they felt that they had failed at
- picking positive experiences, but only, or largely, seeing the negative within them once they began to look at them more closely.

All of these factors undermined the 'neutral', 'detached' examination of their lives that we felt the course structure seemed to be demanding of them. For example, the LET exercises seemed to assume that the students were working with already-processed experiences; that the passage from 'what I did' to the formulation of 'general competences' would be a smooth one. However, many of our students seemed to get caught up in emotional turbulence between the two stages. Even although we had anticipated some difficulties with the material, the strength of feeling that was provoked was striking.

We presented our analysis to the group at the beginning of the following session. The group then brainstormed their fears, feelings and doubts about negative experiences, and considered ideas for group solutions for dealing with them. These were then recorded and displayed in this and all the sessions that followed. The strategies included:

- allowing students five minutes in pairs at the beginning of each class to share feelings that might have arisen during the week

- having a 10- minute open forum at the end of each session to share anything from the class itself
- asking the group for 'space' to 'unload' over a particular issue
- being able to leave the room if feelings became too overwhelming.

We also discussed the availability of support networks for the students outside the class.

It appeared that the process of confronting these feelings was as useful as the actual solutions in enabling students to carry on with the course. (For example, no one felt it necessary to leave the room at later stages of the course.) The process of discussing and identifying reactions reassured students that they were not alone, and created a space for understanding them, not as aspects of individual pathology but as consequences of the social construction of women's identity. Our perception of the group was that the women were very supportive of each other and could therefore gain reassurance from each other as much as from our role as tutors. Because of our previous experience with women-only groups, we had anticipated this; and we trusted also that our pedagogic method had helped enable it.

During the next few weeks, work continued on reflecting on experiences. The material was still largely drawn from the LET workbooks but we modified these in accordance with the women's needs. *The General Learning Checklist* (Handout 7) was a case in point. We extended the skills areas in order to include more space than was originally given to explore women's particular skills areas. The intention was to move beyond the examination of specific experiences in order to look at categories of skills across a much broader range. The checklist also provided an opportunity to examine the 'relevant language' with which to translate skills into categories that employers and education institutions would understand. This exercise, however, proved to be alienating to the students and prompted a discussion regarding the problems in 'marketing' oneself.

By the sixth session, the students were able to re-examine their original objectives for the course (personal development, improving job prospects, etc.) and consider whether they had changed in terms of aims and intentions. By this stage, all of them had formulated clear and realistic long- and short-term objectives. They also all agreed upon the importance of personal development as a key objective, whatever the other 'outcomes'. They had acknowledged the importance of this element of *intrinsic motivation*, without which it would have been more difficult to deal with the harsh realities of the larger economic factors which were informing their lives.

The last few weeks were largely devoted to portfolio preparation and development. We discussed further examples of eliciting skills and providing evidence for them and utilised a case study, also taken from LET, in which an APEL student had demonstrated her problem-solving skills in relation to her choice of primary school for her son (Handout 9). The exercise appealed particularly to those of the students with the fewest formal qualifications. We, however, felt ambivalent about the use of this particular study because after the expenditure of much work and energy the student was accredited with the seemingly banal competence: 'can use observation and judgement in solving everyday problems'. No further evidence was provided as to what the demonstration of that competence enabled her to do in terms of gaining employment – a fact which our students were obviously keen to know.

Dynamics and Outcomes

Throughout the rest of the course, we ensured that time was always allowed for group sharing of the positive and negative feelings about portfolio writing. Once again, it was clear that students found that examining their past could be painful as well as occasionally joyous. One student described the sadness in looking at her past as a 'form of grief'. It seemed, when she looked back, that she saw only the person she had been, and thought of the qualities she had had when younger as 'lost' to her. As the course progressed, however, she became able to reclaim these qualities. Thus, her encounter with the past was not a dismissal and a farewell, but the forming of a new relationship with it.

The positive atmosphere that had been generated during the course was particularly evident at the final session. The evaluation questionnaires emphasised good feelings about the group. The comments included the following:

- meeting some very courageous and talented people
- gaining confidence and recognising and appreciating skills. Discovering shared experiences and feelings with others therefore reducing feelings of isolation
- it lessened my feelings of having failed in the job/career market
- it was immensely reassuring to be in a non-competitive, women-only group and to realise that other people have faced similar difficulties in work situations.

From the core group of students, two obtained places on Access courses for entry into HE the following year, and one on a pre-Access course. One student, having attended adult basic education classess for some time previously, was planning to take GCSE English the following year. Another signed up for further courses in improving educational skills. One became pregnant. One obtained part-time employment as a teacher, another began working with reflexology.

Facilitating APEL

The time-scale for our course was partly determined by the availability of funding and partly by our own inexperience in estimating the amount of time needed. As may be clear from the preceding discussion, we moved almost immediately – and too quickly – into an examination of individual experience. A more impersonal and implicitly theoretically informed approach might have enabled us to avoid the panic and pain that our students went through when they first began to look at their own experiences.

What we have learnt, therefore, is that in future teaching we will ensure that we have an initial introductory session in which there would be no requirement for the students to reveal any potentially painful personal details, but in which we would spend more time in general discussion about informal learning and the ways in which women's skills and experiences receive little social recognition and credit.

There is a hidden gender bias in much of the material so far produced for APEL students. One of the ways in which it makes itself felt is in the notion of experience with which it operates. This is often largely dependent upon 'work' experiences (i.e. paid employment) which have limited application to women who have spent more time working, unpaid, at home. It demands a stance of detachment which may well not be appropriate for all students; and in particular for women who are being asked to examine areas of their lives, such as motherhood, which cannot easily be divorced from personal identity. Where it deals with the 'public world' of work, the skills that are being examined are those which are already valued socially; women, on the other hand, are in many cases confined to the devalued domestic space.

Confronting Personal Experiences

The course could not have had anything like a successful outcome without time having been made within it for the expression of grief about personal experiences. Even positive experiences were revisited with pain, precisely because they were in the past and seemed, for a while at least, to have been lost. One student spoke of the grief and regrets that emerged powerfully for her while compiling the portfolio. Maggie Humm (1989) suggests that men in the process of autobiographical writing (and a portfolio is a form of autobiography and therefore, to some extent, a fiction composed about oneself) find it easier to be future-oriented; women, she suggests, take a heuristic approach, looking in the process to retrieve a past and a truth about themselves. (For a fuller discussion of these issues, see Chapter 2 of this volume.)

We feel that we could have spent more time directly linking individual experiences that were being shared to the wider context of a society divided on the basis of race, class, gender and sexuality. Although we did not wish to polemicise, connections between personal experience and the general experience of women could have been made clearer. We tended, perhaps, to concentrate upon the uniqueness and individuality of the group members without pointing out how our commonalities related to the wider social structure. In essence, we focused too much on 'how you feel' and not enough on 'how we are made to feel'. There is a tension between assessing personal experience and a feminist pedagogy, where the former takes experience to be located within the individual and the latter seeks to question how that experience is socially constructed. Feelings of failure and inadequacy cannot simply be overcome by revaluing experiences in an individualistic way, but need to be examined in relation to the lack of recognition of the multiplicities inherent in the domestic space.

In our pedagogic practice, we wanted to avoid the boundary-blurring between education and therapy that many APEL practitioners seem to advocate. Therapeutic interventions in an educational context are, we believe, dangerous; they can begin processes which cannot be dealt with fully within the framework of a course. This was stressed in our training course, although we rejected the solution of having a counsellor on hand if necessary. We felt that this was disempowering to us as tutors and implied a lack in the course which we felt it was never part of our brief to supply.

During our own course, we emphasised the fact that we were not trained counsellors and that the course was not therapy. Instead, we tried to take a political rather than individualistic and therapeutic approach. We felt that real empowerment would come through students gaining strength from each other, and making links between the personal and political; rather than relying on the tutor as the 'nurturing' facilitator, as some APEL literature suggests. Our experience, particularly in dealing with the issue of negativity, suggests that this approach can be very fruitful and that we could have taken it further.

Addressing Women's Skills

As with the notion of experience, so there can be seen to be a systematic devaluing or invisibility around women's particular skills within the material produced for APEL. There is usually insufficient space for traditional skills such as typing, knitting, cooking. We also added aspects of women's work which are more concerned with personal interaction and negotiating relationships, such as ideas of 'criticising constructively'.

There are also many questions yet to be answered about the assumed neutrality of the concept of skills. Before women can see their experiences as skills, they need to be convinced of their own worth. One student had worked for Amnesty International and held a recognised qualification in the form of a degree; yet she did not put any value on her achievements.

What is Distinctive about MEC?

From the outline we have given, the course may seem to be little different from the kind of assertiveness training and confidence-building courses that have been the staple of feminist education for many years. The most distinctive feature marking its difference would therefore appear to be the portfolio. Many students remarked how glad they were that they had finished the course with something which, even if not complete, would give them something to look at in times of confidence-crisis, as a reassurance of achievement and a source of fresh perspectives on experience which could be the basis of job applications. Yet creating the portfolio was not as straightforward a process as it is assumed to be in APEL materials.

Many women felt that they did not have permission to take their lives and their needs seriously enough to spend 15 weeks on them. This feeling, which emerged in the first few weeks, surfaced again, very strongly, during the portfolio development sessions, which required the students making their 'selves' the focus. Again the 'objectivity' which the course seemed to demand was an issue and fed into the negativity the women felt. Giving oneself credit for domestic competences is very hard when they are taken for granted and rarely broken down into their constituent 'skills'. It was a student who came closest to helping the whole class understand what was at stake when she described how her partner had once tried to make an omelette:

> *First he spent ages peeling the potatoes. Then he put the water on to boil – of course, I would have put the water on while I was peeling them, but he just didn't have those organisational skills. It took ages, doing things one by one; then finally he came to make the omelette itself, looked in the fridge and turned and said to me 'but there aren't any eggs'!!!*

The women also found it difficult to make time outside the class to work on their portfolios. Partly this was due to a reluctance to make time and look at their lives, but it may also have reflected the fact that for them the domestic space was one of work for others, not one of quiet reflection for themselves.

We have already noted that all the students had personal development as a goal which co-existed alongside, and underpinned, other aims to do with advancement in education or work. It follows from this fact and the ethos of the course that students should be able to participate in the process of portfolio development at the level at which they feel happy and confident. The results in terms of the portfolios that were produced, therefore, were widely divergent. One student, for example, ended the course with a finished product aimed at enabling her to gain access to higher education. It contained essays, letters, collages and references, and was beautifully presented, with elaborate hand-drawn title pages. (She did subsequently present it at interview but recounted how difficult the interviewer found it to cope with!) Another student, whose aim was to gain the confidence to proceed further in basic education, concentrated on examining her skills in relation to motherhood, from which she produced the following summary in her CV:

Unpaid Work Experience

1987 – present: Full-time mother and housewife.

Responsibilities include: planning and preparing nutritious food; creating comfortable home environment; providing necessary care and nursing in times of illness; planning cost-effective ways within family income to provide housing, clothing, nutrition and entertainment; ensuring upkeep of home when necessary, decorating, repairing, renovating; managing transport; liaising with doctors and teachers; developing and sustaining social – friend/family – relationships through socialising, correspondence and telephone contact.

The case for employers recognising the transferability of such skills has yet to be argued. In addition, disparities between portfolios may give rise to the making of comparisons which could cause anxiety in some students. The goals of self-development and gaining employment may not be compatible; portfolios developed for the first purpose will not necessarily transfer to the second.

Student Evaluation

The students' evaluations included their often ambivalent feelings about the amount of talk that went on in the course. From our point of view, it was the talking that enabled the group to support each other and to be productive, to see individual experiences as shared and therefore to feel more confident about them. We saw talk as a process of the collectivisation of women's voices, and it appeared to us to be a positive aspect of the course in which we had deliberately allowed space for sharing. Our students' reactions, however, were varied. Some felt as positive as we did and named as the strengths of the course:

- creating around the women themselves and not limiting it to a certain time; flexibility to students' ideas
- having discussions and being able to talk about our personal feelings
- group discussion was valuable for the exchange of ideas and the support engendered by sharing.

Others wrote comments which varied from irritation to a retrospective devaluing:

- perhaps tutors could be more active in disciplining chattering women (of whom I was one)
- sometimes you let individuals rattle on too much
- I think some people rabbited on too long, possibly me sometimes
- too much time on individuals saying their piece
- too informal.

Such comments contradicted our feeling that, although it was hard to confine their talk, we did intervene to keep women to the point and to link discussions to the specific aims of each session. These comments make clear that women themselves do not value their own talk, and also that they felt that we did not fulfil their expectations in giving a firm structure. It might have helped, therefore, if we had explained our style of tutoring more explicitly at appropriate moments during the course. In addition, it is true that the aim or objective of talk is not always clear; there is no immediate positivistic outcome pedagogically, which is not a problem for us, but might be for assessors. There are problems with an educational ideology that is so seemingly product-focused, as the process which informs the product cannot be measured for the purpose of assessment.

CHAPTER EIGHT

Making Experience Count With The Long-term Unwaged*

Education nowadays is all right for computers, but it doesn't open the human being, it doesn't expand the consciousness, it doesn't nourish the soul or the spirit (Kathleen Raine, Guardian *interview, 23 March 1993).*

This course was held at a local Adult Education Centre in Kent. The WEA had enjoyed a positive and supportive relationship with this Centre and had collaborated on a number of developmental projects in the past. We are particularly grateful to Richard Dunn, the Head of Centre, and his staff for their practical encouragement and heartfelt commitment to the needs and aspirations of the adult learner. I am also grateful to Richard for providing extra financial support to the programme which enabled us to employ two tutors for this course.

Jenny Cross, Val Stirrup, Richard and I met on several occasions to discuss the implications of facilitating MEC for the long-term unwaged. Our course was not accredited and did not conform to the vocational criteria required for any NVQ award. We were concerned that our potential students might be misled by our pre-course publicity into assuming that the programme would enable them to obtain employment. It was crucial, therefore, that all our materials were specific about our aims and intentions and did not engender false hopes and promises.

With these concerns in mind, the tutors articulated their intentions in the following manner:

* *Written with Jenny Cross and Val Stirrup*

AIM

To enable participants to review past experience and produce a record of the same which can be used for personal advancement.

OBJECTIVES

By the end of this course, participants will have:

- reflected on and identified skills acquired through experience

- produced a portfolio recording and illustrating these skills

- adopted a positive approach to finding employment

- used the strength of the group to dispel the feeling of isolation endemic to the unwaged

- established realistic goals

- regained confidence and self-esteem.

Partly because of the extra financial help provided by Richard, we were able to offer the programme, with two tutors, over an initial 10-week period at two-and-a-half hours per week. This was then extended for a further two weeks.

One of the issues around working with the long-term unwaged is the problem of assuming a stereotypical homogeneity and pre-empting the needs of the students with facile presumptions about their 'state of mind' and relative levels of 'failure' within our economic and educational system. The danger in this approach is that it can lead to a simplistic 'class-based' analysis of societal inequity with a concomitant denial of some of the acute problems suffered by individuals who do not fall within the more obvious category of the 'disadvantaged'. My intention throughout has been to make space for the voices which are usually silenced, or distorted, by their distance from the discourses of influence which inform our economic, political and gendered social system. Once again, I am reminded of the complexities inherent in the social constructions which shape our responses to 'who' and 'what' we are.

One of those constructions is expressed in terms of societal 'success' or 'failure'. Our latest economic recession has resulted in untold numbers of erstwhile 'successes' tasting the bitter fruits of 'failure' for the first time. This factor gives another twist in the tale to the banality that 'adults are what they have done'. Such a formulation is hardly helpful to those who are no longer 'what they have done' and have to deal with the other side of the equation which means that, therefore, they 'no longer are'.

Course Recruitment and Content

Sixteen students attended the first session. Their ages ranged from the early twenties to the mid-sixties. Some had never gained employment, others had pursued careers in hairdressing; with the Civil Service; and with the navy. Some held degrees, others had no formal qualifications. One family who had lectured abroad had returned home in the hope of finding work. They were, in the words of one of the tutors, particularly anxious at the first meeting: 'Despite their many qualifications, or perhaps because of them, they were highly embarrassed at their unemployed state'. Of the three men who began the course, only one completed the programme.

As the course progressed, the number of regular attenders was reduced to nine. The reasons given by those who left in the early stages included ill-health, family concerns, and a renewed commitment to continuing a personal writing project.

The format of the course followed the pattern of other MEC projects discussed in this book and it would serve no purpose to repeat that outline, in detail, here. The first few weeks were concerned with eliciting the learning gained from the students' experiences and translating it into 'competences'. In one of these later sessions, one of the tutors was being observed by an external moderator as part of the requirement for the successful completion of her ACSTT Stage One Certificate (Advisory

Committee on the Supply and Training of Teachers). Her personal account of this session is illustrative of the anxieties the tutors felt about this process of translation, even if the students were unaware of them:

> *C. came to observe me. Repeated competence statements on board. C. detected our unease with them; she is right, I don't think we are totally convinced as to their point – no, not point – it is as if something is just eluding us. We filled the board with the skills needed to make a skirt, for example. Then seemed unsure what to do with the information – class seems happy, but then they trust that we know what we're doing.*

Whereas the Brighton project had invited specialist input from the careers service, this course invited one of the workers from the Kent Educational Guidance Service (KEGS). The WEA had enjoyed a good working relationship with KEGS since its establishment within the county. The staff employed a similar 'student-centred' approach to the needs of the adults it dealt with, and we were assured of a useful and informative meeting. After this session, the students were better able to formulate their long- and short-term goals, and could begin work on their portfolios. (This excellent organisation has been the victim of 'rationalisation' and has been superseded by a Careers Service almost totally preoccupied with the vocational needs of 16–19- or 25-year-olds.) We are grateful to Jenny Wyatt and her colleagues for their help throughout the MEC pilot.

This group was also fortunate in being housed within a supportive environment. The tutor noted:

> *The room was very spacious, giving every opportunity for both a variety of group work settings and individual working space. The resultant mobility of the class soon created an informal yet busy working atmosphere, with each individual quickly becoming a part of the group. As the course progressed, and various job-search skills were explored, the access to office, television and video equipment proved to be a*

*great asset in the production of CVs, and greatly facilitated
role-play exercises in interview techniques.*

Of the nine students who completed the programme, all
but one produced a finished portfolio. One had gained employment as a Teaching Assistant, one had begun a course in British
Sign Language, one had secured a place on an Access course at
the university, one was seeking an appropriate Access course to
enable her to train as an occupational therapist, one had applied for admission to a welfare and social studies programme
at the local FE college, one had acknowledged the degree to
which her particular nervous condition was inhibiting her life,
and had resolved to seek professional help. She was also the in-
stigator of regular meetings with group members after the
course finished. One had not reached any conclusions about her
future sense of direction but had been short-listed for a job with
a housing association. The only man who completed the course
had asked if he could train as a tutor for future MEC courses.
(He has since completed this training.)

So, in the final analysis, how successful were the original
aims and objectives of the course in meeting the needs of the
students? The following accounts are taken from their end-of-
course evaluations.

Question: What has this course meant for you?

*I attended the course as for quite a while I wanted to do
something other than just being a wife and mother. The
Assertion Training Course I attended gave me an appetite for
wanting to learn more about myself and others and I feel
experience really does count, and that we learn and grow
from it. So when I saw the leaflet advertising the course, I
thought I would attend as I knew I wanted to do something
with my life, but I wasn't sure what. The course definitely
helped me find the route I am now going to take. I really
don't think I would have gone the right route without the
help of the course. I am now very excited and looking forward*

to my new adventure and hope to get employment at the end – a job that will be helping others and hopefully one that I will enjoy. It will involve studying, which worried me, but the tutors have given me the confidence to study again.

The course showed for me what I'd done in my life and that I'd done something and how to make the best of it. I learned more about myself. The course was relaxed so everyone got on great and it was interesting. It was different to anything I've done before, it was new and I met some nice people and it showed me how to make a portfolio.

I joined this course after seeing an item in the local paper about it. I thought – why not? I've got nothing to lose. But I didn't expect to get so much out of it, it's boosted my morale no end. The course has made me realise the importance of things that I thought were just everyday tasks of life that one does just in order to survive, plus the skills we learned from enjoying things, like hobbies and voluntary work or raising a family and keeping a home. It's also shown me how to use those skills and advance them further. It has given me more confidence generally and I have since applied for a job that I know I wouldn't have considered beforehand because I would have thought myself underqualified formally, whereas now I realise that practical skills are just as important.

This course has made me realise that I, in fact we all, have far more skills than we give ourselves credit for. A lot of these skills are, in fact, transferable to many aspects of life and to more than one career. It has increased my self-confidence, whether this was an objective of the course or not. It has made me aware also of the need to present myself in a more positive and clear way.

I took an active interest in class with all the activities and discussions, frequently 'saying my piece'. This was encouraged and I often came away feeling quite wonderful. I felt strongly that I had at times something worthwhile to say and my confidence was hugely boosted when I was listened to *and indeed agreed with. I do not have the portfolio of others as I personally do not want to show one without formal qualifications or work experience. However, I clearly know how to write one and as soon as I have some qualifications, I shall produce my own with enjoyment.*

I have enjoyed the informal atmosphere of the course; I prefer it to a more formal structure where people may not feel so free to speak ... Personally I found that I could relate to the tutors much better because they were women. The majority of us were female so I think it was an excellent idea to have female tutors. The course showed me skills I did not rate as skills.

Question: You met and worked as a group. What are the advantages and disadvantages of this approach?

I enjoyed working in a group as you can share each others' experiences and learn from them and also help each other to discover qualities which, when one's self-esteem is low, we don't tend to recognise. I find working in a group very enlightening and productive.

Working with people helped me so that ideas that I had we could make them even better as a group and we could help each other ... It's also nice to work on your own, have your own space to decide what to do and [it] helps you think for yourself.

To start with I've enjoyed meeting these people. I felt at the beginning that some had far more formal qualifications than me and I felt slightly inferior, but then I realised that they admired my practical skills as much as I admired theirs. I felt to work as a group a particular advantage because of the encouragement that we could give each other. Plus we could relate to each others' experiences and past problems and learn from them ... I really can't think of any disadvantages of working as a group because we all had more than enough chances of individual attention.

Working in a group has the disadvantage that people tend to be a little reluctant to bear their souls in group situations – but once the group has settled down it can be useful, in that people tend to draw courage from each other and relax. Unfortunately, the more reticent in the group do tend to sit quietly in the background and not contribute to discussions – and the group leaders must guard against this sort of thing. Small friendship groups tend to form within the main group and these help by being supportive and encouraging.

A group structure is essential in my eyes, we have fed off each other, watched and heard other ideas and followed each others' hopes, applications and paths. It is as [part of] a group that my confidence has risen.

I think it was very important to meet as a group. One of the main advantages for me was that it got me used to communicating with people again, after being unemployed and meeting no one. Being part of a group simulated a work situation and will give me confidence to relate to colleagues when I do get a job. Also, it was very therapeutic to meet people 'in the same boat' and we have definitely helped each other. Perhaps the 'helping' is more important than the 'being helped', as it is easy to feel useless as an unemployed person. Possible disadvantages are that only a certain amount of individual attention can be given. But I did not find this a problem – everyone's needs were catered for separately but within the group.

Question: Please comment as freely as possible on any improvements we could make when we run this course again.

Have a longer course, more help to deal with personal stress in jobs, e.g. coping with difficult workmates – confidence to approach senior staff. More guidance towards work possibilities.

I found the course enjoyable and informative, it was conducted in a friendly, relaxed atmosphere and the tutors handled the group skilfully. Everyone seems to have got positive results and to have gained in confidence. The mock interviews needed more preparation and it would be an advantage if someone unfamiliar to the group could be persuaded to conduct them.

I would have liked to have been slightly more structured in class, i.e. stopping/starting for breaks at the same time each week, more formal perhaps, but that is just me. The tutors were wonderful: warm, friendly, encouraging, knowledgeable and so 'normal'. There was never a pedestal or a feeling of you/us, I felt as one and as good as my tutors. I couldn't fault them. Seven to 10 people is just right, two tutors made it work well, we all interacted together and I feel two tutors are needed.

I think the course worked very well indeed. I have looked forward to coming along each week and have always gone out afterwards feeling confident enough to do anything. I do think, though, that it could last for longer than 10 weeks, so that certain things could be explored in greater depth – for example, perhaps a session where people were helped individually with portfolios could be useful; perhaps also another chance at a mock interview, with everyone preparing properly for a genuine job vacancy or course. But the reason why I came on the course was to increase my self-confidence and I think that this has certainly happened. It is the only place I have been that concentrates on skills and experience gained outside paid working situations, and this has been very inspiring to me.

We were fortunate in being able to use the success of this course in order to generate funds for two further programmes at this locality. Ironically, in winning the battle for funding, we lost the struggle for students. Neither the tutors nor Richard and myself were able to offer again the amount of time that we had devoted to establishing the first programme. Although we were just able to support the second course, the third was closed on the first day because there were too few students to warrant the funding.

When we talk of the need for support, for monies and for space and time to meet the needs of students such as these we must not overlook the needs of the (largely) part-time workforce that we employ to maintain our provision. We could not have recruited for any of these courses without the hundreds of unpaid extra hours that all our tutors worked – in advertising the programmes, in writing articles for newspapers, in visiting Job Centres, estates, community centres, in liaising with careers and guidance workers, in juggling the demands of their own other commitments in order to continue providing a service to the community. Just as we are often guilty of regarding the 'long-term unwaged' as an homogeneous group and subsuming individual needs in overarching analyses of the 'disadvantaged' and 'dispossessed', we are also in danger of rendering invisible the needs of many of those whose hours of employment are subject to the vagaries of the educational market. The boundaries delineating the full- from the part-time workers and the unemployed are increasingly blurred. Once again, the political and economic assumptions upon which our society articulates its codes and practices are far removed from the realities which inform the major parts of our lives.

CHAPTER NINE

APEL and Admission to Higher Education

Linden West and Wilma Fraser

The Province of the Saved
Should be the Art – To Save –
Through Skill obtained in Themselves –
The Science of the Grave (Emily Dickinson # 539)

Introduction

In 1991, the University of Kent (UKC) was one of six higher education (HE) institutions to take part in a pilot project co-ordinated by The Learning From Experience Trust (LET) and funded by the Department of Employment. The intention of the project was to encourage the use of APEL within admissions procedures.

A full account of the process is available from The Unit for the Study of Continuing Education at the university (see bibliography).We are grateful for their permission to include this version here.

This chapter is concerned with highlighting one particular set of issues – the difficulty in adopting a facilitative approach to translating experiential learning into a very specific public realm: assessment for access purposes within HE.

Whereas work of this kind has been taking place within the former polytechnics for a number of years, most university initiatives in this field have been promoted by continuing education (CE) departments. These introductory notes are therefore couched in a language particular to the concerns of extra-mural – now more often referred to as CE – departments.

The difficulties encountered during this project have raised fundamental questions about the different discourses which operate in adult education and higher education. There are a range of differences of which practitioners in both fields are acutely aware. These may be summed up in the following problem. How to marry adult education traditions of empowering educationally disenfranchised members of our community with an HE system which is fundamentally predicated upon instilling academic excellence within a societal elite? It will be argued that the demise of the binary line and government avowals of increasing access are indications of a fundamental and paradigmatic shift away from such a traditional distinction. This is the issue that many CE departments are now grappling with.

We are still at the transition stage between the old culture and the new. Government-funded Enterprise Units have been established in some HE institutions with a view to developing 'transferable skills' which will better prepare adults for the world of work. These units have not necessarily been placed within CE departments, partly, we suspect, because the formers' emphasis on improving the marketable skills of graduates and postgraduates is not necessarily seen as consistent with the ethos of the latter. The extra-mural tradition was originally conceived as a means by which the cultural riches within the walls of academe may be made more available to those who, like Jude the Obscure, would be forever otherwise denied them. Of course things have changed since then. CE programmes today are as likely to include professional courses and those for vocational advancement as they are programmes within the 'liberal tradition'.

But the point at issue is not just about kinds of courses on offer and whether they are vocational or liberal; the point is the nature of the curriculum and the way it is taught. And it is precisely these issues which departments of continuing education should be encouraged, and enabled, to explore.

APEL represents one method by which such questions are highlighted. Knowledge, within our Western tradition, is regarded as 'objective', subject-based, transferable from expert to recipient and ultimately quantifiable in terms of what Lambert (1987) has called 'culturally shared test procedures'. APEL, if it is to fulfil its potential as a student-centred, problem-solving process, will inevitably clash with our traditional phenomenology of knowledge and education because it addresses the issue of what it means to be 'qualified' for higher education, thus challenging the very concepts of 'excellence' and 'exclusivity' upon which HE has always rested (e.g. Usher, 1989).

We are not suggesting that there is anything wrong with notions of excellence. We are arguing that at this particular juncture, when CE departments are struggling to maintain both identity and purpose, they are, in fact, best placed to claim centre stage in articulating and debating these very issues which are at the core of our concerns for the future of adult and higher education.

Two people are credited with writing this chapter. Wilma Fraser was the course tutor for the project and Linden West, Lecturer in Continuing Education at UKC, was the manager. However, we worked as a team and our reports have also been conceived as joint explorations. This chapter is no exception.

The Course

Getting the balance right requires careful consideration of questions such as who controls the procedures, who makes the decisions about what is required and what constitutes satisfactory evidence of competence (Bainbridge, quoted by Usher, 1989).

The course was offered as part of the admissions process for part-time degree and diploma courses which are administered by UKC's School of Continuing Education (SCE).

It was considered unwise, at this stage, to contemplate introducing APEL within the mainstream admissions procedures. Kent is one of the most popular universities in the country and can rely on a plentiful supply of conventional applicants. However, the lessons learned from the pilot were to be used as a means of challenging traditional entrance criteria at a later date.

The project was divided into five distinct stages:

- recruitment of students
- interviews with admissions tutors
- a staff development day
- the course itself
- further interviews with tutors to assess the validity of the process.

A further evaluation day was planned for the students after they had embarked upon their programme of study. Unfortunately, this proved to be impossible to organise; and one of the disappointments of our course has been the impossibility of monitoring our students' progression into HE.

Recruitment

The APEL course was highlighted in some 2,000 brochures advertising the part-time diploma and degree programmes and the SCE's Access courses. Conceived as a 'fast-route' access option, it was to run for four full days, totalling 20 contact hours, spaced at intervals to allow for reflection and portfolio preparation.

The description of the project's aim was 'to help adults to identify those experiences in their life which have developed their academic abilities'. The examples given included informal learning gained at work, in pursuance of a hobby or in voluntary or community service.

Of the 50 people who made enquiries, 40 came for interview and 12 self-selected for enrolment. Of those who did not comprise the 12, many opted for a full one- or two- year Access programme. Given that the course was offering a 'fast-route' access option it was a pre-requisite that students knew which programme of study they wished to pursue *before* the course commenced – how else could we articulate their experiential learning 'as a match' to the requirements of particular disciplines? Thus, those who opted for an Access course did so because either they were unsure of what to study or judged themselves unready, as yet, for the rigours of academic work.

Before the course began, the students were asked to complete questionnaires designed to probe motivational factors as well as elicit personal and educational histories – the research was conducted by Mary Telford, UKC. The results confirmed research findings elsewhere (Woodley *et al.*, 1987; McGivney, 1990). Like Access students and adults on qualification-bearing courses more generally, the APEL participants were relatively young in comparison to adults in, for example, liberal adult education programmes. Four were in the 26–35 age bracket and six in the 36–45 group. Only one was male. Four participants had been divorced, reinforcing findings that life crises may be significant factors in prompting moves to educational participation.

Two of the students described themselves as being in managerial positions, two as housepersons, while the remainder classified their occupations as skilled or semi-skilled; one was unemployed.

Everyone had known some 'success' at school and half had stayed on after 16. With two exceptions they had participated in a range of post-school and adult education courses and six had acquired qualifications in relation to their careers or voluntary work. Two of the students were currently attending 'Return to Learn' courses. The experience of adult education was no doubt reflected in the response to a question about what they looked for in education. They wanted learning to be different from school, with 'no indoctrination', 'no patronising attitudes', and an environment in which 'an adult should have no need to enforce the right to question'. Despite a relative ignorance of the APEL process, they anticipated and expected learning to be student-centred as well as to stretch and stimulate them.

What about motivation? There was a persistent theme of needing or wanting to change either personally, professionally or both. Most indicated that change was desirable and that their motives, although clearly occupational, were deeply personal as well. One student, the man, was the exception; he considered the idea of personal and professional change to be inappropriate in his case; he was choosing to study 'for its own sake'.

There are a number of issues here which directly address broader concerns of 'access' and 'opportunity'. We have noted that the students on this course were 'typical' Access students; they had all enjoyed a fair degree of success at school and had continued with a conscious pursuit of learning in other forms, formal or informal, for vocational or leisure purposes. Thus, the perennial debate about the degree to which 'access' is a misnomer is introduced once again.

There were two barriers to inclusion on our course. The first excluded all those members of the community who would not leaf through an Access brochure because they would regard HE as an educational option forever closed to them. The second barrier was the more exclusive requirements of the APEL course itself. It was not available as a diagnostic space for assessing future directions. Students needed to know which discipline they sought and they had to have enough self-confidence to believe they could attain entrance to that discipline within the very short time available.

Although we would urge the need for APEL-type provision precisely because there are students who do not need a one- or two-year Access course, it could be argued that we were erecting a further barrier by providing a course for students who would previously have asked for informal interviews and been accepted for direct entry. In other words, what has been termed the 'A-levelisation' of Access has prompted fast-route alternatives. But are they effective alternatives or yet more barriers?

The ratio of women to men on the course, and the responses to questions of what had motivated them to enter HE, is in accord with other research findings. However, there are issues here which point the need for far greater understanding and analysis. Although it is a truism that personal crisis is often a motivating factor in prompting applications to HE, it is interesting to note that the desire to change was most often expressed in career terms. Personal reasons were included in this, but the combination of desires at this particular time in women's lives is in accord with certain findings which point to a need for self-advancement and independence, i.e. greater involvement in the public realm, on the part of women when they reach their late thirties and early forties. This is often in contrast to what research into male motivation has found; a desire to eschew the public realm and enter what has been termed 'a generative phase' (Sheehy, 1974; Levinson, 1978). We need more research into comparative life-cycles because most adult learning theory has been based on studies of men. An exception is the work of Belenky *et al.* (1986), whose explorations of *Women's Ways of Knowing* provide a much needed spur to an area of research which could radically affect the fortunes of the mature returner, female or male, were there a clearer understanding of their differing motivations and expectations. These issues are explored in greater depth in Chapter 2.

Interviews with Admissions Tutors

Five admissions tutors in literature, history, philosophy, social policy and women's studies programmes were interviewed – before the course began and after the applicants had decided which course they wished to pursue. The purpose of the interview was four-fold: to introduce the concept of APEL, to establish the criteria tutors applied when selecting applicants, to reflect upon the competences devised by course selectors in an earlier LET study (Handout 8), and finally, to consider the form and focus that portfolios should take. It was interesting to note the similarity of their responses. They agreed that it was important to broaden access opportunities and viewed APEL as an interesting tool in this respect. When asked to comment on their current assessment practice, the response was almost always an acknowledgement that without recourse to standard criteria, 'A'-levels, Access, etc., it became a matter of 'intuition' or 'gut reaction'. The following quotation, although taken from one of the more extreme responses, nonetheless illustrates the point:

> *What comes to me is a slight surprise that this sort of thing hasn't been done long before now. When I think of the interviews with other social scientists but also with humanities specialists, they can be tremendously unstructured or foolishly structured exercises.*

Most welcomed the opportunity to reflect on their own practice and urged that some method of 'skills equivalence' or 'generic competences' be structured or documented to enable them to judge their candidates more 'objectively' and thus more fairly.

They pointed out that lack of time precluded detailed analysis of a lengthy portfolio and asked for two to four sides of A4, which would suffice to indicate the level of skills attained and their relevance to the student's desired discipline.

There was an emerging contradiction between the aims of the project, the wider needs of the students, and the requests of highly sympathetic and committed but uncertain tutors. It has been argued elsewhere that APEL is not always primarily about identifying the learning gained from experience and proving its applicability in another context. It is also, and perhaps more importantly, about recognising the intellectual rigour and commitment which is required in undergoing the process and regarding that as proof of academic ability (see, for example, Hull, 1992). Herein lies the problem – for how is that proof to be evidenced except as a piece of written work which, in turn, will be assessed for its structure, its analysis and synthesis; in other words its ability to objectify the learning gained. And so we note that accreditation or assessment in the public realm, and for a particular purpose, will invariably mean incorporation of the process, or at least its outcome, within the discourse to which the process is applied.

We have already noted the differences between APEL in this context and the broader MEC programmes described elsewhere in this book.

The Course Philosophy

Perceived as a 'fast-track' option, the aims of the course were, by definition, circumscribed. The students had elected for particular programmes, the relevant admissions tutors had provided guidance as to their requirements; this would necessitate eliciting students' competences and expressing them in a language consistent with academic requirements. But how was this to marry with our commitment as a team to student-centred learning? APEL, we believed, should be rather more than a crash Access course devoted to improving writing or textual criticism, important as these skills may be.

APEL provision takes many forms. Whether a student works alone or in a group situation will depend largely on the resources of the institution attended. The project at UKC was conceived in group terms and group activities influenced course planning. If a sense of common purpose can be generated at the start of a course, an integrated group dynamic can provide support and encouragement and perform an integral function in increasing self-confidence.

Warner Weil (1989) has elucidated the various strands that together inform a valuable learning experience, and one which goes some way towards alleviating the sense of alienation and 'disjunction' that earlier mis-educative experiences might have produced:

> *an overall sense of integration itself in connection with academic learning programmes includes the following: the active use and appreciation of different forms of knowledge (e.g. experiential, tacit, practical, propositional), the making of connections across disciplinary boundaries, and a positive valuing and use of personal and social differences within a group.*

Warner Weil's research shows that women in particular value peer group support although the dynamic can sometimes be double-edged. A dominant individual may silence the less-confident and reinforce feelings of worthlessness and isolation. However, if part of APEL's challenge to the dominant educational paradigms is the acknowledgement that learning is also constructed in relation to others then, on balance, the group approach would seem the more rewarding. There is another and related issue which is also to do with confidence. APEL as an individual process, via for example, a distance-learning package, is extremely difficult to undertake if there is no support to assess the reality of one's starting point. We would argue that this is an issue for women in particular, because women tend to undervalue our prior experiences, thereby failing to do ourselves justice.

Another factor which informed the course's content was the decision to incorporate study skills. Acceptance on a course is not the same as preparedness for it. Methods of note-taking, of skim reading, of verbal and written reporting, as well as timed exercises and simulated seminars, were all highlighted and their effectiveness reflected upon and judged by the students.

It could easily be argued at this stage that little appeared to remain of APEL as a learning process-in-itself. How did this differ from any study skills unit which incorporated confidence building?

The Materials

The coursework was based on the materials available from The Learning From Experience Trust. Other sources included readings relating to the experiences of the mature student, an analysis of group dynamics and our own teaching materials which formed the basis of a jig-saw reading exercise.

The Participants

Of the 12 who initially enrolled, illness, change of plan and a late return from holiday reduced the course complement to nine – eight women and one man.

Course Format

The course was held over a period of four days and totalled 20 contact hours. Students were expected to complete several hours of home study in the intervals between contact days which were spaced between a few days and a week apart.

The aims of the course were as follows:

Day 1
1. To foster a common sense of purpose and a positive group dynamic.
2. To acquaint and familiarise the students with the distinctions between formal and informal learning.

3. To introduce the concept of the 'transferability' of informal learning to formal learning through the medium of 'general competence statements'.
4. To begin the task of matching tutors' requirements to the skills the students already possessed.
5. To practise the skills required; elicit information from a text (skim read), take notes, communicate verbally.
6. To introduce the need to distinguish between different levels of attainment in preparation for home study and Day 2.
7. To evaluate Day 1.

Day 2
1. To pursue our understanding of the levels of competence required by admissions tutors.
2. To begin the process of linking the students' experiential learning with the language required by the admissions tutors.
3. To facilitate written work by elaborating upon a personal experience (non-threatening) via the medium of different levels of vocabulary.
4. To try, therefore, to minimise the threat of sophisticated academic phraseology.
5. To simulate a study seminar in order to familiarise students with differing discursive methods and purposes, and to reduce the potential anxiety induced by unfamiliar group dynamics.
6. To evaluate Day 2.

Day 3
1. To reduce student anxiety regarding evaluation of their written work by encouraging peer assessment and thereby reduce the authority of the tutor's judgement.
2. To simulate a second seminar group with the tutor as facilitator for comparative purposes (see Day 2).
3. To evaluate Day 3.

Day 4

1. To provide a sense of completion/*Gestalt* to the course process.
2. To analyse and practise note-taking as a study skill: what function does it perform?
3. To further progress written work
4. To provide simulations of forthcoming interviews for practice and analysis.
5. To evaluate the whole course.

Content

(For a full account of the methods and materials used on Day 1 please refer to Chapter 4; see bibliography for handout details. The 'I' in the following account is Wilma Fraser, who tutored the course.)

The first day began with paired introductions to elicit partners' names, the course applied for and why. This was fed back to the whole group and followed with an alliterative name game. I then asked the group to brainstorm what was meant by 'learning'. In two columns, the students then tried to distinguish between 'formal' and 'informal' learning. Their results were compared with Handout 6. The next stage was crucial – how to distinguish between an 'experience' and a 'learnt experience'. Kolb's cycle (see Chapter 1) was used as a timed experiential exercise and the students discussed their feelings and the difficulties in moving from feelings to reflections to theorisations. I then elicited the problem with unstructured learning, which is that it lacks formal proof. In other words, how do we translate 'What I Did' to 'What I Learnt' to 'Possible General Competences'? Handout 3 was studied and discussed within the group. Handout 7 was then used as a means of individual self-assessment.

The students then used the material to work through one life event and compile a progression from 'What I Did' to 'Possible General Competences'. The results were discussed in pairs and the partners added to each other's lists. One student was then asked to share with the group and the others were invited to add to the list on the board.

The next stage involved the transference from student competences to admission tutors' requirements. It was noted that Handout 7 included some general competences that were suitable for university entry. In subject groups of twos and threes the students compiled a list of assumed requirements on flipcharts, rapporteurs then invited additions from the other groups. The results were compared with Handout 8, which had already been discussed with the admissions tutors. The comparisons were, gratifyingly, almost identical.

To effect a change of tempo, and to introduce the study skills element, I then led the group through a jig-saw reading exercise. Each student received a series of questions and a section of text which would provide answers to only some of the questions. In a timed exercise the students had to skim read the relevant material, take appropriate notes and then seek out the other answers from the rest of the group. The general feedback was then concerned with how the students had coped, and more importantly, how they had felt. The day concluded with the acknowledgement that admissions tutors were not only looking for 'competences' expressed in 'demonstrable outcomes' but for evidence of 'levels of achievement'. The students were given Handout 10 and asked to continue with the exercise of expressing their learning but incorporate, if possible, the different levels of vocabulary. We wouldexamine how those different levels reflected distinct academic levels (and expectations) on Day 2. The day was then evaluated in plenary.

The second day began with a discussion of the students' process and progress with the home study. We discussed the uses of vocabulary levels (i 'knowledge', ii 'interpretation', iii 'application', iv 'analysis', v 'synthesis', vi 'assessment') and the common experience of seeing a film was used as a group exercise to create a paragraph using the vocabulary levels of i–vi above. The students then constructed their own paragraphs and discussed these with a partner.

This was followed by a general discussion to elicit more general skills required for written work from their own job/personal experiences. The students were then asked to prepare one side of A4 for the third day.

The study skills element took the form of a simulated seminar. Reading material was handed out and the students were given time to note the main points for the later discussion, which would be student-led. One student volunteered to act as facilitator and the others were asked to monitor their own participation (or lack of it). I acted as observer. The group dynamics were then explored and participatory methods discussed. The day concluded with an evaluative feedback session which included student needs for incorporation in Day 3.

The third day began with a discussion of fears and feelings about the process of committing oneself to paper. It was agreed that different types of written work required different frameworks, e.g. academic essays, work reports, personal memos, etc. The group were split into twos and threes to share and constructively criticise their colleagues' work. I visited each group, checked progress and process but tried to resist the role of final arbiter. The students were asked to complete their final drafts for the next session.

Because of the unhappy experience of the previous simulated seminar (see Evaluation) the process was repeated with fresh reading material and the tutor acted as facilitator. Once again, the group dynamics were explored and the participatory methods discussed. The day concluded with an evaluation and an agreed outline for Day 4.

The final day began with a study-skills element. The group debated reasons for and methods of note-taking. Each student then elicited which of the following three 'types' to join: 'frantic scribblers', 'selective' note-takers or those only allowed five minutes at the end to summarise. I then read an article concerning group dynamics and illustrated certain points on the board. The students then re-grouped and compared notes and levels of understanding. The feedback concerned previously held assumptions about how, and why, to take notes, and their efficacy or otherwise. The article's relevance to the course was then debated, and the students returned to further peer, and tutor, assessment of their written work.

It had previously been agreed to hold simulated interviews with Linden West, the project manager, who role-played both the 'unsympathetic' and the 'encouraging' admissions tutor. Individuals volunteered to undergo this process whilst the rest of the group observed and then offered feedback. The day concluded with an evaluation of the whole course. The students were asked 'what and how to evaluate' by considering what they felt the course's aims to have been. These were discussed in plenary and I asked for written assessments to be sent to Linden. The completed assignments were collected. The rest were to be sent, within the week, to either the relevant admissions tutor or to Linden.

Evaluation

This course attempted to integrate three basic approaches:

- to alleviate the tensions between student-centred learning and academic requirements
- to foster a cohesive and supportive group to generate confidence and aid learning
- to incorporate study-skills – as practice – in order to reduce student anxiety when faced with the rigours of the HE programme.

Was it realistic to expect these processes to be achieved over the course of four days?

Day 1 was necessarily tightly constructed. 'Ice-breaking' exercises and sharing the reasons for applying to HE did engender a sense of common purpose despite the fact that those applying to the same discipline assumed that they would be in direct competition for places.

The use of Kolb's cycle as an experiential exercise to establish the differences between formal and informal learning proved an effective method of providing an emotional underpinning to cognitive understanding. By then working through personal (non-threatening) experiences to understand the learning gained, and by sharing these with a partner, the students soon grasped the immense potential in reclaiming those experiences, and regarding them as valuable and self-affirming. It is important to note that APEL, by working through 'life events', will obviously regard painful experiences as 'grist to the mill'. Earlier experience of facilitating experiential learning had taught us that without a considerable amount of time and access to a counsellor, if required, it is inappropriate to highlight painful material as a source of learning. This is not to say that students will not want to discuss issues if they arise, and if they feel safe to do so. But the tension between reclaiming personal experiences, 'owning' them and then proffering the learning gained to the scrutiny of the public domain provokes serious issues of moral responsibility. Selective use of, e.g., LET material and carefully guided exercises can provide the boundaries between a 'course' and a counselling programme. Many colleagues would disagree, arguing that responsibility for disclosure lies ultimately with the student. This is not in question. But to use APEL as a 'fast-route' to Access imposes its own constraints, of both time and expectation, and care for the student must be of paramount consideration. (For a discussion of the deeper issues involved, see Chapters 2 and 3.) Even within these constraints the group dynamic is potentially explosive, as will be seen.

The shift in emphasis, on the course, from the personal experience to the general competences required by the admissions tutors at a time when the students were feeling confident proved immeasurably beneficial when the group split into subject areas to try and decide what the entrance criteria would be. The clarity of their responses and the match with the tutors' stated requirements added an extra confidence derived from the sensation of meeting academia on its own ground; the students were engaged with the task in hand.

Therefore it seemed appropriate at this point to introduce the study-skills element. The jig-saw reading exercise provided an opportunity to tackle academic texts and measure performance. The material was chosen for its relative difficulty and the exercise could have proved disastrous were the students overawed by a lack of understanding. Fortunately, their confidence not only enabled them to complete the task successfully but to tentatively begin to question the authority of written material; 'I don't agree with these conclusions because ...' were rewarding statements for both student and tutor alike! The day ended with a resounding sense of accomplishment.

In the intervening four days until the next meeting, the process of reflection and consolidation had obviously been of particular importance emotionally. As already noted, the experiences discussed and shared were not of themselves necessarily emotionally charged. The resonance came from a sense of the uniqueness of those experiences. But consolidation of those feelings, whilst bringing about greater self-confidence, also prompted an understandable reluctance to see them transferred, piecemeal, to a different sphere which would then render them subject to another's judgement. The necessity of transferring 'competences' to the academic arena began to meet resistance during Day 2.

The main area of contention was the length of written work required. The admissions tutors had requested between two and four sides of A4. Some students expressed a wish to complete a 'full portfolio'; why should they be limited to what others deemed acceptable? The confidence to engage with academia on its own ground was now leading people to express doubts about the whole enterprise. There was increasing tension between the need to 'play the game' (and win a place) and the need to prove that the 'game' itself was highly suspect. This tension deserves closer inspection.

On the one hand one could argue that the group had become a victim of its own success. We were extremely fortunate to have gelled so effectively from the outset. The potential for a sense of 'disjunction' had been superficially dispelled with the ability to question academic authority. This, in turn, had given way in some to an understandable anger that, 'if this is all there is to it, why has it been denied me for so long?' Hence the feeling that there was a game to be played and that the rules, once mastered, would admit access. But challenging a dominant and exclusive system is not the same as battering at its walls, and perhaps I, as tutor, must take some responsibility for 'allowing' this slippage. It was a consequence of the struggle between 'owning' and 'being judged'. But was it inevitable? The students' sense of confidence, too, being so recently expressed was still quite shaky and so an increasing tension began to manifest

as heightened competitive, even aggressively individualistic behaviour on the part of one or two, with a growing confusion as
to the 'nature' of academic authority on the part of the less secure.

The exercise to elicit and analyse 'levels of learning' and incorporate these with 'levels of vocabulary' proved particularly
interesting at this point. The lists, although developed by the
LET, are thought to derive from Bloom's taxonomy of educational objectives. Usher (1989) is not alone in expressing anxiety
about the reductionism implicit in their behavioural bias:

> *Since learning has to be stated in terms of 'unambiguous'*
> *performance statements, the assumption is that if one cannot*
> *do so, then no learning has taken place. But must learning*
> *always be performatively statable and demonstrable? ...*
> *(Why) the emphasis on an 'appropriate' terminology of*
> *'action verbs'? This could become a strait-jacket where*
> *finding the right word assumes the status of a ritual which*
> *must be gone through at the expense of learning.*

Once more we confront the issues of who is in control, who
makes the decisions, and what constitutes satisfactory evidence
of competence? As we have already noted, the admissions tutors had not previously considered the nature of the competences required. Any negotiations undertaken were certainly
not the result of institutionalised procedures, and yet here we
were offering a taxonomy of learning skills as if they were the
key to creative intellectual attainment. We could not have been
further from validating the prior learning of our students; so,
what had become of them, and of our 'process'?

Given the tension described above, was it perhaps paradoxical that the 'levels of learning' exercise was greeted with a
measure of relief? It was as if the straight pedagogic intervention at this point provided a comforting realignment of old expectations and therefore old responses. The work was taxing,
and that was to be expected, after all access to HE was an extremely difficult barrier to overcome. And so, as the students
worked hard to incorporate more 'sophisticated' phraseology
into their written work, it seemed, at this point, that it was only

the tutor who fretted about whether real learning was taking place!

The quality of the written work itself was also causing some concern. Without having seen examples of work from the various diplomas and part-time degrees, I was struggling with the conviction that two or three of the students would not be able to produce work of 'a suitable standard'. Once again, where was the yardstick, and who was doing the measuring? The problem was exacerbated by the fact that the diplomas applied for were not all of the same level. This is a point discussed in more detail below.

Consistent with the apparent paradox that the need for an authority figure became more acute as the questioning of 'who can judge' became more explicit, was the experience of the following exercise. I had chosen to simulate a student-led seminar. This proved to be a mistake. Few students participated fully; some even behaved with a truculence reminiscent of high school. It was only by analysing the dynamics afterwards that a degree of group cohesion was restored and some support given, in retrospect, to the student who had led the discussion.

This central paradox – awareness of, resentment of, resistance to but need for 'the rules of the game' – ebbed and flowed throughout the rest of the course. The open-ended potential and enthusiasm generated on the first day seemed now limited, restricted and targeted on improving written work and dissecting and analysing the 'good and bad habits' of other study areas and skills. If the purpose was to facilitate entry to HE then it were best effected by tutor-led methods. My intention throughout had been to maintain confidence by demystifying certain alienating aspects of a higher educational institution. I wished to minimise resentment of another's 'right to judge' by placing initial response within a structure of peer support and constructive criticism. The students resisted this; whilst accepting peer criticism with a kind of detached politeness, they regarded the tutor as the only and final arbiter in matters of what would 'pass' and what would 'fail'.

The second simulated seminar was more 'successful' in that it was more focused because it was tutor-led. However, it provoked little real engagement because the reading was judged of little interest, despite having been selected for its apparent relevance to the group.

At times the pace of the course and the tensions outlined above provoked an understandable irritation towards the tutor, who persisted in trying to maintain a facilitative rather than authoritative posture. We would like to think that the more student-centred approach prevailed, indeed even cite the frank discussions and ease of interchange as evidence of a reasonably egalitarian relationship. However, this, in turn, provoked another anxiety. Would the attempt at a student-centred, student-led course have much relevance once the participants found themselves within a more traditional academic framework? For this reason, it seemed particularly important to effect a 'closure' to Day 4. The APEL course, although a process and with ongoing resonances, had to be seen as distinct from the 'reality' of the academic institution. The mock interviews, conducted by a relative outsider, provided a suitable change in perspective; away from the APEL programme and towards the next step.

A final word needs to be said about the completed assignments. There had been a certain dissatisfaction about the length of written work required. Nonetheless, half the students submitted work of the statutory two to four sides of A4. Three others, all of whom were applying to the social policy department, decided on the final day that their previous experiences were of sufficient academic equivalence to merit 'advanced standing'. These elected to submit their portfolios within the week, having added further arguments to support their case. A further student, applying for the joint literature/philosophy diploma, was absent during this discussion. Encouraged by his wealth of prior reading and obvious intellectual ability, we decided to explore the possibility of 'advanced standing' on his behalf.

Unfortunately, there were institutional difficulties – the status of the diploma did not necessarily enjoy sufficient cross-disciplinary equivalence to render exemption from Part 1 an easy matter; the possibilities would be explored at interview. Yet another student, applying for the women's studies diploma, had already been offered a place after an advisory interview which had taken place during the APEL course. She was still expected to complete a written assignment because entry for this diploma was considered equivalent to entry to Part 2. For the other crucial factor in trying to facilitate access for our students was the fact that UKC, in common with some other HE institutions, did not have a coherent policy with regard to the levels of its various diplomas. It is to be hoped that modularisation will effect some degree of coherence across the institution as a whole.

Admissions Tutors' Responses to the APEL Process

We negotiated a second series of interviews with staff after the course had finished.

The four candidates for one course found that the tutor we had spoken to initially no longer had responsibility for admissions. The replacement knew nothing about APEL and had time merely 'for a quick glance' at the work before making her decision. She could not comprehend the worth or the point of portfolios and it is hardly surprising to report that no applications for advanced standing were taken seriously. Fortunately this was not the case with the majority, who declared themselves convinced of APEL's value. One interesting example of the way in which prior experiential learning was seen as 'transferable' was the account that one student gave of the process of analysing her own divorce. The admissions tutor noted that the student had shown aptitude in retrieving information, criticising texts and producing a coherent narrative, however painful the context.

Another tutor was honest about the more general problem of admitting mature students when there was no lack of conventional applicants. He regarded it as a 'moral choice' between a place for the former and a place for someone with 'A'-levels. On balance, he argued, the judgement would tend to be one of 'who is going to do best?' The tutor was not necessarily in favour of younger or conventional applicants but acknowledged that ageism might reflect his feelings that 'Access people' – in their thirties or forties – may struggle. Therefore the potential

APEL group 'is a group about which it is most difficult to make a judgement'.

The Students' Responses

Most of the APEL participants were offered places, although, as we have seen, not necessarily at the level they would have liked. One decided to delay entry for personal reasons and another was offered a place on an Access course. In the case of two others, personal circumstances changed and they were unable to take up the offer of a place.

Their response to the APEL course and its aftermath varied. It is hardly surprising that one described the admissions process overall as 'a mystery which I still don't appreciate. Disjointed and unco-ordinated'. The verdict on APEL itself was, predictably, mixed. On the positive side there were a number of comments on the value of APEL as a tool with which to bring together work – i.e. vocational – and academic abilities. It assisted a number of the students to appreciate the commitment involved in HE study and 'the sorts of level we would be working at'. The benefit of being helped with essay writing techniques was mentioned, as was the practice in seminar and discussion groups. There was appreciation of the simulated interview because it had helped in dealing with the reality and alleviated a certain amount of anxiety. But there were also useful criticisms, and, again unsurprisingly, they reflected the issues which have already been noted as being of particular concern.

> At the beginning I thought we were to write a portfolio and be guided through the best ways to present ourselves within it and at interview. Towards the end of the course I felt it became much more general and was unsure of the aims.

One participant thought that the students should have been given examples of different possible components of a portfolio, including, for example, 'an extended essay, an essay with *curriculum vitae* information attached, a work report, a critical essay and a piece of creative writing'. The second major criticism concerned the role of the tutor. As we had thought, some wanted more direction. One person felt it would have been better to have been provided with an agenda, although she wanted it known that she felt the presentations were good.

Briefly, the anxieties reiterated the fundamental issues that this chapter has been attempting to illustrate. The students resented the possibility that the wholeness of their experience might be distorted in a short piece of writing or that academics would sit in judgement on what they, the students, had only recently discovered, and valued, in themselves.

Concluding Remarks

It was noted early on in this chapter that it was concerned to highlight one particular set of issues – the difficulty in adopting a facilitative approach to translating experiential learning into a very specific public realm: assessment for Access purposes within HE.

The danger of treating parts of an individual's experience as unworthy, or of ignoring aspects because they are considered irrelevant to HE, is real. It seems that when students discover new or previously undervalued skills they want to own the realisation for a period and are reluctant to have the learning assessed. There is an acute tension, as Usher has observed, between the essentially 'private activity of reflecting on experience and the public activity of having the learning from that activity publicly assessed'. It is important to remember the types of students in the Kent study; many were in transition personally and professionally and feeling vulnerable as their past, present and future were reconsidered. It is not surprising that strong emotions were consequently released. Neither is it surprising that when insecurities came to the fore, there would be a consequent reaction to the facilitative method we were trying to employ.

The problem lies in trying to move beyond the vicious circle that this kind of work so often finds itself caught within. Can the process ever be different, given the fact that APEL in this context is part of a selection procedure and that procedure, as was also evidenced in this discussion, will dictate the limits of its own discourse? Not everything that has been learned will be relevant to the ability to write a clear narrative, to synthesise from many sources, to apply and evaluate different theories; in other words, to realise detailed competency statements. On the other hand, students naturally want to say something about the context in which they have learned. And it is often crucial to know how an individual acquired certain skills: the situations, on close scrutiny, may be analogous to those which students will find in the academy. There is a danger of relevant material being lost in standardisation and arbitrary limitation.

The question is once again one of 'relevance'. How are we to assess the value of 'competences' when the tools by which they might be assessed may themselves be reductionist and simplistic? How are we to match tabulated 'levels of learning' with the complexity of the learning process itself, and the creative interplay of the myriad of cognitive, experiential, spiritual and ethical factors that inform true learning?

Where are the incentives to begin to truly grapple with these issues? Of course, things are changing. If the HEFCE decides to set quotas for mature students, if the moves towards modularity also provide a stimulus to the development of APEL, then we may see these issues taken on board as issues for the institution as a whole. But if being 'taken on board' means the further formalisation of practices such as APEL, as academics call for standardisation and equivalence, then the truly radical nature of APEL's challenge to the academic mainstream may be lost in institutional mishap and misunderstanding.

We did not do APEL justice at UKC. We can blame time constraints and our own fuddled approach. The alternative is to conclude that our traditional phenomenology of knowledge and education is still relatively safe from the student-centred and process-oriented approach that APEL tries to offer. Indeed, perhaps such an approach is ultimately misguided. But now is the time for continuing education departments to take the lead in addressing these questions and their implications for HE as a whole.

The Story So Far

I gave up career ladders long ago.
Instead, I make a patchwork, intricate,
with patterns that accumulate and show
paths chosen, chances taken, twists of fate.
With every change I add on something new:
a velvet, tweed, lace, cotton, cambric spread,
with colours vivid, fading, gleaming, true.
I will not finish it till I am dead
and the last stitching eases into place,
an unexpected edge, the quilting lined;
I'll leave it with you, one last deep embrace.
And you can tug it straighter in your mind,
smooth out the tuckered bits of cloth, and see
myself, complete. As I turned out to be.

The Quilt, *Jan Sellers*

This section describes our work with MEC in the WEA South Eastern District since the pilot project was concluded. That programme had depended upon the seed-corn monies provided by the national WEA's development fund. Our intention, from the outset, was to continue our MEC provision by generating funds from a variety of sources based on the success of our initial endeavours.

There were three main reasons for wishing that the work continue. The first, and most obvious, was that we believed in the value of the process despite the concerns that this book raises. The second, and related, reason was our commitment to maintaining a form of provision which was specifically targeted to those members of the community who would not usually regard adult education as relevant to their needs. The third reason concerned our responsibility to the part-time tutors we had trained and their own commitment to the continuation of the MEC programmes. It would be a pity if the tutors did not have the opportunity to 'make sense of the experiences' they had undergone as facilitators by exploring some of the issues in further courses. At a personal level, I was also acutely aware of the investment that the District had made in terms of the time I had spent on the project. I felt the need to justify that expenditure by proving the viability of MEC in the long-term.

Our first problem, therefore, was to secure sufficient funds to cover all the costs of the classes. We could have chosen to place MEC courses within our mainstream liberal programme and charge for attendance in the usual way. But our commitment to the 'disadvantaged' meant providing courses which were free. We also wished to collaborate with other educational providers. Apart from enhancing our chances of generating money, collaboration was essential if we were to offer a programme which had credibility within the county, given that our MEC courses were excluded from the Kent Access Consortium and given the fact there was then no Open College Network in the county to offer an alternative means of accreditation.

This section relates the brief history of the Kent APEL Consortium from its establishment to its untimely demise within a few short months. It then includes an account of our recent work with MEC set against the vexed question of accreditation.

This section concludes with a description of a new initiative for us – an MEC course designed for the needs of women within the Punjabi community in North Kent.

CHAPTER TEN

The Politics of APEL: The Kent APEL Consortium

We are all of us born in moral stupidity, taking the world as an udder to feed our supreme selves: Dorothea had early begun to emerge from that stupidity, but yet it had been easier to her to imagine how she would devote herself to Mr Casaubon, and become wise and strong in his strength and wisdom, than to conceive with that distinctness which is no longer reflection but feeling – an idea wrought back to the directness of sense, like the solidity of objects – that he had an equivalent centre of self, whence the lights and shadows must always fall with a certain difference (Middlemarch, *George Eliot, 1871–2).*

The Kent APEL Consortium was established in March 1992 to further the work of the assessment/accreditation of prior experiential learning in the county.

I had initiated the Consortium as a means of bringing together representatives from each of the educational sectors who worked with adults, and who wished to explore APEL's potential as a means of promoting educational opportunity.

Our first meeting included representation from the University of Kent, The Open University, Mid-Kent College, the Kent Educational Guidance Service, the Adult Education Service, Kent County Council and the WEA. During preparatory discussions with these colleagues, I had stressed the need for a forum which acknowledged a distinction between APL and APEL in terms of both rationale and delivery. Some of these colleagues already attended another forum which had been established by one of the FE colleges to explore ways of collaborating in the expansion of APL. I had also been invited to the inaugural meeting but had been dismayed at the emphasis upon linking APL with NVQ. Once again, I felt alienated by what I perceived to be yet another articulation of the prevailing economic discourse. It was the fact that others shared my anxiety that prompted my belief in the need for an alternative space in which we might explore our concerns, and, by naming them, perhaps formulate another discourse with sufficient weight to attract the kind of support that would allow our work to continue.

At our first meeting I circulated my reasons for the establishment of our group:

It is important to distinguish between APEL and APL in order to consolidate the range of work undertaken by educational providers in Kent and thus avoid needless repetition from already scant resourcing. APL is concerned primarily with the assessment of competences gained from the workplace or accrediting/certificating agencies. The results might be proffered towards the awarding of NVQs or other forms of certification. APL has the support of certain government funding because it is seen to be linked to measurable outcomes. APEL seeks to include the learning derived from experience – whether formal or informal – and regards the process of reflection as the key to realising the potential in transferring life competences to other, more specific areas. Competences are seen as generic life skills which can be utilised in any number of formal or informal situations; APEL, therefore, has been accepted by some HE institutions as a broad-based Access equivalent. Completed portfolios are submitted for direct entry or advanced standing (i.e. exemption from parts of degree or diploma programmes).

Because of the general and broad-based nature of much APEL work, 'outcomes' are not always measurable in the terms currently understood by funding bodies – they might not result in NVQs. However, pilots undertaken by the WEA in Kent, in conjunction with the LEA, careers guidance, UKC and social services, have shown marked improvements in the confidence, self-esteem and clarity of understanding of the students. These factors have, in turn, resulted in the greater potential for employment or further education. Many of our students have now gained new employment or places within an academic institution.

Therefore the Consortium has been established to:

(i) Discuss issues of mutual concern, and further research into the nature and implications of reflective learning processes.
(ii) Lobby funding bodies to enable the work of the pilot projects to continue.
(iii) Increase APEL's profile within FE and HE; urge its equivalence to Access within the Kent Access Consortium and work towards its emplacement as an admissions tool within HE and FE institutions.

Our first meeting was spent in examining the range of APL and APEL provision in the county. The WEA pilot projects had involved the adult education service and the University of Kent. I had also met with some FE colleagues and explored the possibility of running a joint APEL programme as part of their college's admissions process. What was particularly heartening about this inaugural meeting was the participants' willingness to share their concerns and future plans despite the fact that each institution or organisation was in a competitive relationship to the others in terms of students, funding or both. Indeed, what began as an analysis of current APL/APEL practice and a discussion of our different approaches soon developed into an exploration of our underlying frameworks of belief and our shared commitment to educational process and student-centred learning.

I am not trying to claim that the individuals gathered round the table at that meeting were the only educators in the county to share the same concerns and a similar ethos. Neither would I wish to suggest that discussions about relative 'ownership' of the learning process were not taking place in other forums and other institutions. Yet this meeting felt different. It was as if the members had come together as individuals who were participants in a broader educational enterprise – one that eschewed institutional boundaries and the narrower agendas of particular organisations. I believe that the Kent APEL Consortium was born out of a collective need to *communicate* at a deeper level than was usually possible in meetings convened to effect the business of educational delivery.

This feeling stayed with me during our second meeting three months later. There had been worrying political changes in the interim and the Kent Educational Guidance Service (KEGS) was about to be subsumed within the careers service. This would mean the demise of a form of provision specifically geared to the guidance needs of adults as opposed to school-leavers and those up to the age of 25. The meeting was cheered by the words of our colleague from KEGS who was moving to the careers service yet wished to retain her commitment to the APEL Consortium and remain involved in any collaborative activities.

Indeed, we felt strong enough as a group to begin to devise strategies for approaching the Kent Training and Enterprise Council (TEC) to secure funds for a county APEL project. I had met representatives from the TEC on a number of occasions but had always been greeted with the same response. Our work in the WEA was obviously of value to the students but unless we could guarantee NVQ outcomes, the TEC could not furnish us with any money. We trusted that the APEL Consortium might be viewed more favourably because of the range of providers it represented. It was agreed that my task before our next meeting was to formulate a paper couching our proposals in a language appropriate to and commensurate with the TEC's brief, yet falling short of any promise to generate NVQs.

It was also felt advisable to approach polytechnics and universities as soon as possible in order to benefit from the imminent demise of the HE binary line. With so many institutions adopting a modular approach, it seemed that now was the time to negotiate APEL for Access with our local HE providers. We debated one of the issues intrinsic to the relationship between experiential learning and academic qualifications – how to equate notional time spent on study with the competences gained – and acknowledged that we needed a broader framework within which to introduce the value of APEL. Although a forthcoming Kent Conference on Accreditation and Open College Networks had been postponed, we decided that we need not wait for a local Open College to be established but should forge links with either the London or the National Open College Federation. There was much to be done and, it seemed to me, we had both the impetus and the commitment to succeed. We agreed to meet again in three months' time.

At the same time as establishing the Kent APEL Consortium, my WEA colleagues and I had managed to secure funding for further MEC courses. The story of these programmes forms the basis of the following chapters. What is important for our current discussion was the fact that by the time we met again, the number of 'graduates' from our MEC courses had reached over 80. Our success in maintaining the provision encouraged our belief that it was time to meet with the TEC and discuss the possibility of submitting a collective bid to enable us to promote MEC/APEL throughout the county at a number of different venues. Our arguments were summarised in the following points:

1. MEC 'graduates' now number approximately 80.
2. The 'outcomes' are known – several students have been tracked and their progression routes include FE, HE and employment.
3. The pilots were successfully targeted. The project can claim considerable success in having reached sections of the community which would not normally avail themselves of educational/vocational opportunities.
4. The successful outcomes of the courses argue the case for supporting ventures which are not strictly limited to the awarding of NVQs. Many professions are not yet NVQ accredited, the parity of NVQs and other qualifications has not been finally formalised, yet we are putting people through a system which is of benefit to the individual and to the larger community, which has achieved tangible results, but our funds are limited.

We decided to make the following proposals:

THE POLITICS OF APEL

(a) To secure funding for a two-year period to enable:
  - APEL training for the WEA/LEA/FE, etc.
  - the continuation of the kind of courses already established
  - the financial support to encourage pump-priming of ventures currently in the pipeline.
(b) Funds to explore new possibilities, e.g. pre-redundancy packages, pre-retirement courses.

It was now September and the start of a new academic year. We scheduled our next Consortium meeting for November, by which time three of us would have had discussions with the TEC. Our conversations were still frank and free-flowing. We lamented the pace of educational change in the county and the fact that increasing pressures were making it more difficult to sustain provision at the margins. Our Local Education Authority was being restructured yet again and our Chair had recently been appointed as head of the new Kent Adult Education Service (KAES). This meant that her time would be even more limited. We began to talk of establishing a core group which would have responsibility for furthering the actions decided at the meetings and then use the forum for report-backs to the larger membership.

In October three of us met with a representative from the TEC. In November we held our fourth Consortium meeting. The restructuring of educational provision in the county was now beginning to take effect. I shall quote from the Minutes of that meeting (I have referred to the speakers as A,B,C and D):

what remains (of the educational budget) depends on the contractual relationships with the schools – devolvement to schools will amount to up to 95% of the total available budget ...

A. stated that the Kent Careers and Guidance Service was undergoing further reorganisation ...

B. outlined the situation with regard to Continuing Education (CE) departments in HE institutions. £40m is currently spent on CE (including professional and vocational updating as well as liberal education). The New Universities – erstwhile polytechnics – argue that continued funding for CE should not be given separate status because CE was a feature of their mainstream (Polytechnic) provision. Ring-fenced funding will hold until '94/95. After that it is likely that Universities will have to bid through mainstream faculty provision ...

C. reported on the meeting held with the TEC. It had been obvious that there were similarities of approach; what was needed was a translation of our language into that commensurate with TEC requirements ...

There was some discussion as to the role of the APEL Consortium. Whilst members valued the freedom of exchange offered and the space to discuss issues fundamental to the future of adult and further education in the County, it was still a forum with a brief to implement change and further APEL/APL initiatives ...

We decided to concentrate our efforts on exploring the possibility of matching educational equivalences. There had been a recent Further Education Unit project which had examined the relationship between Open College credits and NVQs. We reiterated our interest in and support for an Open College in Kent. It was decided that we should extend the membership of the Consortium to include further representation from the FE sector. The main agenda item for our next meeting would be to discuss the possibility of organising a County Conference on APEL/APL. Our fifth meeting was scheduled for January 1993. In the event, it had to be postponed until February.

Once again, there had been changes in the interim. We discussed the development of the Higher Education Colloquium in the county and its interest in establishing a Credit Framework for Kent. There was concern that its local focus would jeopardise the value of its credits at the national level. We wondered how it could relate to the Open College Network. I cannot recall much of the rest of the business that day, although, as convener, it was my responsibility to take the Minutes. At the top of the page I had written:

> *(Our new FE representative) asked what purpose there was in the breadth of the APEL Consortium representation. He stated that FE and the WEA and Adult Education would sometimes be in conflict.*

I remember his declaring that the frankness of our discussions was surprising, given that there was sure to be much that we would rather keep to ourselves. To this day, I cannot tell whether his presence was the catalyst or the cause of the chasm that opened before us. I cannot remember much of the ensuing conversation. However, at some stage I wrote on my paper that our colleague from the Open University wanted to minute his appeal that the value of the group as a 'sharing space' be retained. I note that now because he never saw those Minutes. I did not send them out. There was no longer any point because the Consortium has not met since.

I regularly come across colleagues from our forum, in other meetings, with other agendas. No one refers to what happened during our last discussion. No one asks why I have not reconvened the group. Perhaps we all know that sometimes we just need to move on.

CHAPTER ELEVEN

'Learning From Life': The Issue of Accreditation

The unknowability of the other inheres not only in the problems I have described – the deep structures of image and language, the individual's intentional and unintentional decision to conceal, the observer's scotomata – but also in the vast richness and intricacy of each individual being. While vast research programs seek to decipher electrical and biochemical activity of the brain, each person's flow of experience is so complex that it will forever outdistance new eavesdropping technology (Love's Executioner and Other Tales of Psychotherapy, *Irvin D. Yalom, 1989).*

Since we began our work with MEC in the WEA South Eastern District we had of course been aware that our courses offered no form of accredited outcome. Our broad-base approach to access meant that we were exempted from inclusion in the Kent Access Consortium (KAC). KAC, as an Authorised Validating Agency (AVA), is subject to national criteria which are now under the auspices of the Higher Education Quality Council; monitoring and control of all AVAs used to be the responsibility of the CNAA. In practice, this meant that our MEC courses could not qualify for recognition because they did not conform to the 'class contact' time required.

There was then no Open College Network in the county to which we could apply for alternative validation. It would have been possible to have worked with our nearest Open College or to have sought recognition from the National Open College Federation. However, the somewhat *ad hoc* approach to our work, based, as it was, on organising programmes when, and if, we secured external funds, spoke against any systematic attempt to adopt a coherent MEC 'package' for which we could seek recognition. As I noted in the Introduction, we believed that our courses were of value in themselves, but we were also aware that many of our potential students would be attracted to courses which offered some form of validation. This was particularly true of those whose previous educational experiences had been negative and had left them without the 'piece of paper' that marked academic success. As facilitators, we were torn between *our* belief in the work we were doing and our acknowledgement that we were operating from a position of academic privilege. *We* had succeeded in the academic mainstream – what right did *we* have to decide on the value of certificating procedures for those who had not had the opportunity to negotiate them? Nonetheless, we continued to run our programmes and the numbers of our 'graduates' mounted. With monies secured from the 'Disadvantaged Funds' of Birkbeck College and the University of Kent we had run several MEC courses for the long-term unwaged.

We also gained support from a local Branch of Barclays Bank, from South Kent Social Services and from Kent's Training and Enterprise Council. Then my colleague David Alfred in East Sussex (which forms part of our WEA South Eastern District) secured substantial funding from the British Telecom (BT) Community Partnerships Scheme to run 10 15-week MEC courses in the Hastings and Rother area. We embarked upon a further training programme and recruitment drive and five MEC courses retitled 'Learning From Life' were completed between November 1993 and March 1994. Two more courses in the programme enrolled in September 1994.

The BT Project

Once again, we worked with tutors who, with two exceptions, were experienced facilitators in community or women's education. Although the BT project could only provide work for those tutors in the East Sussex area, we took the opportunity to invite tutors from elsewhere in the District who had expressed an interest in training for future MEC courses. Our group therefore comprised 10 in all – seven women and three men – of whom six were expected to teach under David's auspices. The programme was conceived on similar lines to the initial training programme described in Chapter 4, except that we did not examine APEL as a 'fast route' to HE, and the outline of the course requires no repetition. What is worth mentioning is the different dynamic that was generated in the group and how this affected the tutors' perceptions of the courses they would soon undertake.

The Training Course

The first training day was almost a repetition of my first MEC training course. I adopted an experiential approach and sought to familiarise the tutors with the process as well as the theory by immersing them in the material as if they were the students and then analysing their experiences as potential facilitators. We worked well together, the atmosphere was mutually supportive and the day ended with a feeling of accomplishment. I asked the tutors to record a journal of the learning they gained from the training course. This would provide an idea of the process we ask our students to undergo when compiling their portfolios, and would also generate an ongoing reflective process which, I thought, could only enhance intellectual and emotional appraisal of the ensuing sessions. What happened in the following sessions represented a micro-cosmic replay of the concerns discussed in this volume. I offer a brief analysis of the issues that arose as I experienced them, fully aware that this is a partial view and cannot possibly encompass the feelings and perceptions of my colleagues.

The reflective process that the tutors embarked upon during the first session and in the days between our meetings had the same effect as it does upon our students. Some spoke of feeling more confident as they began to acknowledge the depth and complexities of the skills they had at their disposal. But some also revisited sites of old pain and distress; memories came unbidden and the emotions they generated were felt as keenly as when first experienced. One tutor spoke of the shock engendered by the realisation that they had not resolved long 'forgotten' events in their life. For some, feelings of increased self-confidence were interwoven with anxiety and disquietude. The resultant volatility of our group 'cocktail' was soon susceptible to the smallest spark. It came in the form of an interchange between one of the men and two of the women.

It would be easy, looking back, to regard the explosion as symptomatic of fundamental gender differences in the way we perceive experience. This was certainly the view of some of the group members. Yet there were other factors informing the dynamic which had equal, if not greater impact upon the ways we related to each other and the MEC process.

Most of the tutors had facilitated subject-based courses – a few had been working with the same discipline for a number of years. They were highly competent and assured of their pedagogic capabilities. To use the MEC argument, they had the generic skills of all good facilitators, the training course would simply be a matter of learning how to transfer these skills to a different arena. But if this were the case why was there so much resistance to the interactive element that MEC as a group practice requires? In some cases, confusion was hardening into intransigence and covert, at times overt, aggression. I could not understand why this training course should be so different from the last; neither did I know how to deal with it.

In retrospect, my response only compounded the problem. In all of my work with MEC, I had not internalised what I had observed intellectually. I had not accounted for the extent to which the nature of what we do informs the sense we make of who we are. These tutors had spent years teaching with and through a subject. But MEC has no subject except the students themselves. I was therefore asking the tutors to abandon the medium through which they had developed their practice; the medium through which they had projected themselves. I was asking them to elicit a subject out of the raw material of people's lives and I was using their reflections about their own experiences as the basis of that process. I do not regard it as surprising therefore that the strongest resistance came from those who had to abandon a subject and replace it with acute self-analysis. The corollary held true. Those few tutors who had not had much teaching experience were much more open, at least on the surface, to the process we were undergoing.

Yet I am also a tutor who has spent most of her working life facilitating subject-based programmes. Faced with the intensity of emotion within the group, I fell back upon the 'material' – my lesson plans, explanations and exercises – avoided directly confronting the problems and maintained a distanced and 'objective' stance. It is hardly surprising that some of the aggression was reserved for me.

The training programme lasted four days. We also arranged to meet once during the course of the tutors' own classes and again for an evaluation session at the end of the project. Five of the six who had originally elected to run the BT courses began their classes; one of the tutors withdrew stating that: 'it is not my kind of teaching because I prefer more structured work.'

The Issues

Given the problems we had encountered during the training sessions, it is not surprising that I was anxious about the tutors' levels of preparedness for the situations in which they might find themselves. What would happen if they encountered similar problems in their own classes? What should I have done to alleviate the tension? How responsible was I for making it worse? In short, how should I have delineated the parameters to my role as facilitator?

The tutors' evaluations of the courses which they facilitated spoke for themselves. Each had recorded an extensive account of their own and their students' processes. What follows is a brief selection extracted from the tutors' written reports and taken from their students' final assessments:

What I have liked most about the course ...

- everyone supporting each other
- gaining confidence and a positive attitude
- finding myself
- working in a small group

- learning how to look at life differently and learning about others' experiences
- working as part of a really supportive team, exchanging ideas and being guided in such a relaxed but progressive way
- the location was ideal, the facilities were excellent
- being able to express my feelings without being undermined by others
- my favourite exercise was talking about dreams

What I have liked least about the course ...

- the homework and realising that my time allocation at home is poor and frequently undermined
- not having enough time for work especially in the last few weeks
- I found the written work difficult – I didn't have the confidence to talk about my competence and skills
- I didn't enjoy the course when the group was large and there was a lot of discussion about children and families
- self-examination made me feel uncomfortable

What I found most useful about the course ...

- gain in confidence and difference in style of job applications
- I now know who I am and why I do the things I do. It has given me confidence to realise that I am in control of my own life
- being able to assess abilities and becoming aware of strengths and weaknesses
- being able to express myself and being able to talk more openly in the group
- location: good parking facilities
- creche

Another tutor wrote:

You will see from the 'Individual Outcomes' section that participants, with one exception, expanded their horizons in terms of:

- *now being happy to attend formal College courses*
- *realising that (my) experience was valid and valuable*
- *making long-term plans and implementing them step by step*
- *producing or updating CVs using experience as valid evidence*
- *producing a portfolio*

Another tutor who was teaching two programmes noted the differences between them:

Although the stated aims and objectives of both courses were the same, the emphasis of the two courses differed. At B. the main thrust of the course was examining experience and extracting 'useful' abilities, knowledge and qualities; whilst at E. the emphasis was more on communication skills (verbal and written) for educational and personal development.

This is how the students articulated their responses to the tutor's questions about what they had learned from the courses:

Now they know ...

- beans are not the only vegetable (!)
- how to deal effectively with the media
- myself better
- how to evaluate past and present experiences more usefully
- how to deal with people in difficult situations
- I can't make paid work a priority

Now they feel ...

- in my prime
- aware and accepting of who I am and what I can do
- less inadequate

- that I understand more about my misconceptions of others
- that I'd like to continue campaigning, publicity work
- that I need to get the family to take more responsibility

Now they have decided ...

- that the future, work-wise, might not be so difficult
- on a computer course
- to find part-time work
- to look for cheaper housing
- to take a degree
- to apply for an adult education course
- to take the first steps
- that I am allowed to choose

It is interesting to compare these comments with those from students on the second of the two courses:

Now they know...

- how to get what I want out of the 'system'
- what a CV is
- myself better
- how to have an argument without losing my temper
- that other people think differently
- that other people have the same problems
- that I don't have to be pushed around
- my rights

Now they feel ...

- better
- clearer
- less in a mess

Now they are able to ...

- speak up for myself

- write a CV
- write a letter
- think before I act

Yet another tutor facilitated a small, women-only group. The following extract is taken from her final report:

From the beginning, the women had a very positive attitude towards the content of the course. They worked hard throughout. The idea of looking at personal or life experiences in terms of learning was a new one, and, I feel, was seen as a very constructive exercise. It took the women (and me) some time to understand how learning could be extracted from experience and we needed to spend quite a lot of time on this. However, once established, we then moved on to extracting personal skills and competences. By and large, the women grasped this exercise very quickly. Again, we spent a lot of time on this aspect of the course, and I really feel it had a very positive effect, enabling women to take a much more constructive and appreciative view of themselves. For the whole of the final block (of five weeks), the women tended to work much to their own pace. By the end all the women had either completed a CV or were in the process of doing so, and also had portfolios well underway. Significantly, as well, some of the women were making specific plans for activities to follow the course ... In addition, I feel women had the opportunity to meet others in the same situation, and to see that new possibilities were available to them – through voluntary work, further courses, or perhaps waged work. This is not an easy course to tutor, there is a constant fine line to tread in using personal experience as learning or skills material, and one woman in particular found personal contributions difficult to make. The idea of waged employment too as being the main measure of status in our society is also a very difficult position to move away from. Nevertheless, the course does present that possibility – in the end it is up to group members to take it up or not.

Experience as Quantifiable

There are a number of inferences to be drawn from the relationship between the events of the training course and the actual MEC programmes. Before discussing these, a word needs to be said about another facet to this project which related to broader issues to do with our provision generally. I have mentioned the vexed question of accreditation. Apart from the concerns discussed above, there was increasing pressure to rethink our position because of the new arrangements by which the WEA was to be funded.

Public funds received by the WEA from the Department for Education were now to come from the Further Education Funding Council. The WEA was to be regarded, for all intents and purposes, as qualifying for the same kind of support as FE colleges. This meant that the same criteria were to be adopted by which we could sue for funds. Of the many categories relating to funding, 'Schedule 2' was one of the most significant because of its inclusion of broad-based Access courses which were recognised by an Authorised Validating Agency. I have already noted that we were excluded from recognition by the Kent Access Consortium but we could apply to an Open College which held the AVA 'kitemark'.

We began negotiating with London Open College Federation (LOCF). It was agreed that we should include MEC in a broader application for recognition. Our contact at LOCF furnished us with examples of similar programmes and we met and discussed the mechanics of their accreditation procedure. These meetings coincided with the commencement of the 'Learning From Life' project. It was obvious that these courses would form ideal pilots from which to develop an MEC 'package' which could then be used anywhere in our District and, theoretically at least, generate funding so that we could continue to provide the courses free of charge.

There was one basic problem. The tensions that had been surfacing in our work with MEC, and which form the basis of this book, raised serious questions about the nature of the accreditation process. We had eschewed the 'outcomes' approach, believing it to distort and reduce the complexities of the MEC experience. Would an Open College approach prove broad enough to encompass such compound diversity?

There was another and related issue. How were we to accommodate the levels of learning that the Open College process recognises? Given that learning stems from the students' experiences, were we not in danger of assessing those rather than the learning derived from them? In other words, and however benign the Open College approach, were we not perilously close to reinforcing a similar 'pass or fail' judgement that so many of our students had suffered from in the past?

There seemed to be only one way to deal with these questions and that was in open forum with the tutors who would facilitate the 'Learning From Life' courses. I was responsible for the development of MEC and broad-based Access within our District but I could not impose an accredited procedure on tutors who were beginning a new programme, and who had already experienced some of the contradictions that the work could entail.

We arranged to hold an extra two meetings to discuss the issues. I circulated the LOCF material in advance and asked the tutors to come to the first meeting prepared to argue the case for and against accreditation. By this time, they had begun their courses. I asked them to include in their assessments the feelings and requirements of their students. Once again, I wished to avoid the situation of making decisions on behalf of those who had not benefited from the educational system in the way that we, the facilitators, had.

Our conversations were frank and extensive. Two of the tutors reported that their students had asked at the beginning of their courses whether they would receive any certification for the work they would do. Yet within a couple of weeks of meeting, they were saying that the process they were undergoing seemed to be important in its own right.

We could reach no agreement. Two of the tutors felt that we should offer accreditation despite our concerns, because to do other would be to impose our own sense of educational 'purity' on others. Another two were categorically opposed to any form of accreditation, arguing that it would diminish the process, narrow the focus and reduce the potential creativity of the experience. They held to this view despite my warnings that failure to accredit might mean that we could lose sources of funding to enable the provision to continue. I pointed out that the tutors might not therefore be employed to run MEC in the future. It is to their credit that this factor did not affect the way they perceived the educational value of the programmes. One stated that we had an obligation, as educators, to fight for the retention of a space in which adults may explore the issues that the MEC process entails. She declared that there was 'precious little left' of the tradition which proclaimed 'education for life, not livelihood'. Under the circumstances, few of us could have remained unaware of the irony lying behind the title of our current project.

We agreed to postpone a decision, rethink our position and arranged another meeting. On that occasion, it was decided that 'Learning From Life' would not be accredited. Two tutors offered to facilitate accredited courses in the future, two refused to teach MEC if it were accredited. The others did not wish to be involved in any form of accreditation but would reconsider their position if it meant that our MEC provision could no longer be sustained: 'It is better to retain MEC in some form than to lose it altogether'.

As the tutor trainer on the 'Learning From Life' project, there were times when I found the process to be painful and frustrating. Yet, in retrospect, I recognise that the problems which arose in the days we spent together stemmed from the same contradictions that are inherent in facilitating MEC in the classroom. Of course, this should come as no surprise. I had adopted an experiential approach to the teacher training and had required the tutors to undergo a similar reflective process to the one they would facilitate with their own students. Why should I assume that tutors would behave any differently with the complexities and contradictions inherent in the MEC process from the adults in their classes?

I also have to acknowledge my own position within the group dynamic of the training course. By retreating behind the materials at my disposal, I was, in fact, attempting to contain the multi-faceted responses of my own students by translating them into a medium for intellectual analysis. I remember, after

one particularly painful exchange, adopting a traditional pedagogic stance and 'lecturing' for 20 minutes on theories of adult
learning. This gave us all pause and, for some, a certain amount
of relief. One tutor commented on the fact that she was so
thankful that, for a while at least, she only had to sit and be
'talked at' rather than 'listened to'.

Was I acting 'in bad faith'? What are the limits to my relationship to the group dynamic; to the students as individuals
and as fellow adults? Some of the aggression was directed at
me. It was articulated in our evaluation session when two of the
tutors said that they would have been 'angry' had they been required to pay for the training. 'There was far too much philoso-
phising, and too little structure ...'

There is another and related issue which has a bearing on
the vexed question of accreditation. I used the same materials
and structure on this training course as I had on the first MEC
training programme. Yet the dynamics had been completely
different. The tutors had used similar materials and structures
when facilitating their own courses. Yet, as evidenced in the
students' 'evaluations', differences arose according to the nature of the individuals in the groups. Is it possible, even with
the generous boundaries provided by the Open Colleges, to devise an 'off the shelf' MEC 'package' that would suit all comers?
A colleague from another WEA District who also facilitates
MEC, and believes in the value of Open College accreditation,
states categorically that she has to formulate a different MEC
application for every group she tutors.

We have just finalised a contract with UNISON to produce
an MEC 'Distance Learning' pack for use throughout the country. The contract states that the material must carry Open College accreditation and one of the original MEC team is to write
the material. But if MEC has to be accredited in order to survive, how are the issues addressed in this chapter to be res-
loved?

*(With grateful thanks to my colleagues: David Alfred, Jill Ayres, Jill
Britcher, Jane Davies, Sue Forward, Wilfred Gaye, Kate Goree, Ann
Kramer, Christine Mackenzie, Joy Pascoe and Derek Sideaway.)*

CHAPTER TWELVE

Making Experience Count Within the Punjabi Community *

'What will happen at the end of the project?' she asked. 'Will there be other monies to sustain this particular development?' (Tutor from the Punjabi Community, April, 1994).

In April 1994, my colleague Jill Britcher secured funding from the Kent Training and Enterprise Council (TEC) to run an MEC course for Punjabi women in North Kent. For three years, we had been negotiating with the TEC for money to fund our MEC provision. The answer had always been the same. The work we were doing was obviously valuable, but we did not offer NVQs as an outcome and therefore the TEC could not support us financially.

What brought about the change in attitude was a combination of factors, including a perceptible shift in the 'learning culture' within the county. The TEC had recently begun advocating a 'Return to Learn' programme which had been concerned with persuading employers that one of the keys to economic regeneration was an educated workforce. The TEC had illustrated their argument with examples drawn from, among others, the Ford EDAP scheme (see Chapter 5). My colleague decided to broach the subject of our MEC provision once again.

We received enough money to fund a pilot project. This chapter relates the story of that project and concludes this account of the development of our MEC provision since the initial pilots in 1991.

* *Written with Sarabjit Mema and Monalisa Webb*

Between April and July 1994, we identified tutors, ran a training programme, recruited students and completed a highly successful MEC course. None of this would have been possible without the support and encouragement of Dot Riley and her team at the Victoria Adult Education Centre in Gravesend, Kent. Dot has been working in support of the learning needs of the ethnic minority communities in North Kent for many years. Her Centre has run an extensive programme of courses for the local communities and she has remained a staunch supporter of the WEA in the region. Dot supplied us with accommodation, with places in the creche and with support from her administrative staff.

However, there were other issues which would have to be addressed if the pilot were to be a success. We had been given an opportunity to test the relevance of our approach within a different cultural context. All our anxieties about the specificity of the material came to the fore; and these were compounded by my own concerns about the contradictions inherent in the MEC process. Nonetheless, we did not wish to forego the chance of extending our provision within a different cultural, in this case ethnic, context. In early discussions with the TEC representative, Jill and I outlined the benefits of the MEC process and the three of us agreed a strategy for providing MEC and meeting the requirements of the TEC.

Their representative explained that the TEC had acknowledged its failure to reach into the heart of the Punjabi community, which was the largest ethnic minority community in the area. If the TEC were to facilitate vocational and educational opportunities in the region, then it had to address the specific cultural issues which affected whether members of that community were enabled to take advantage of its provision. The representative also pointed out her own concern that the community was not utilising the various welfare services which were still available in the area. There appeared to be a reluctance to approach the health services; the TEC representative wished us to include an introduction to health issues on the MEC course so that we could find out where the resistance lay.

Jill, the TEC representative and I agreed on the basic requirements for launching an MEC programme within the Punjabi community:

1. We would have to recruit tutors from within the Punjabi Community. Much of the language in which the MEC materials is written is problematic for the majority culture; it was vital to have mother tongue speakers facilitating the course so that they could translate both language and context where necessary.
2. Ideally, two tutors should be appointed to the pilot scheme, in order to support each other, particularly where cultural issues might limit the support that I, as tutor-organiser, could offer.
3. The project was acknowledged to be an experiment from the outset. Jill and I made it quite clear to the TEC representative that were the (potential) tutors to decide that MEC was totally inappropriate to the needs of their community, then the programme would not run, but the TEC would be given a full report as to the particular problems and how they might be addressed.

It goes without saying that these decisions were based upon the best of our collective intentions.

The first step was to recruit tutors from the Punjabi community. Dot furnished me with a list, and three women began an intensive four days of what I loosely termed a training programme. From the outset, I stressed the fact that the course was a pilot. It represented an opportunity to explore the relevance of a certain type of provision to the needs of a community for whom it had not, in theory, previously accounted. I made it quite clear that the course would not take place if the tutors felt the ethos and the material to be irrelevant to their needs. Thence, the material was under constant scrutiny; more importantly, so was the ethos.

At the end of the first day, one of the tutors stated that she felt that this course represented yet another attempt by the majority community to impose its educational standards on the minority. 'What will happen at the end of the project?', she asked. 'Will there be other monies to sustain this particular development?' Did I not 'represent yet another form of cultural patronage' because I was offering initial educational largesse that would ultimately account for no more than a few weeks of 'outreach work'? I had no response except to stress the sincerity of our commitment and to point out that our lack of funds affected sectors of all our communities. 'Then why target the Punjabi community?' And she asked if I were not aware that most 'development' money was directed at this particular community at the expense of the many other ethnic or linguistic minorities in North Kent. I replied that the TEC had highlighted this particular community precisely because it was the largest and would therefore presumably offer the TEC the greatest potential for assessing its needs and offering the most useful provision.

This tutor left the programme after two days. She assured me that the reason was a misunderstanding about her teaching availability. The other two decided to complete the training sessions and commit themselves to the recruitment and tutoring of a group of women from the Punjabi community. They felt that the main problem about the material would not be its cultural specificity but the level of linguistic ability required to 'make sense of it'. I pointed out that one of the reasons for employing facilitators from the Punjabi community was the fact that they could translate the language of the materials they wished to retain; and could substitute materials which they felt were more appropriate to their needs. The tutors explained that were MEC to succeed within their own community, it could only do so on the terms set down by the majority culture. There would be no point in encouraging the students to work in Punjabi because it would not help them to succeed in the dominant culture. It was imperative that we all acknowledged that working with English as a Second Language would have its place in the course, but only as a last resort. The motivating factor that would bring the women to the programme would be the opportunity to gain useful employment or access to an educational opportunity.

We produced a leaflet advertising the course and one of the tutors had it translated into Punjabi. Both of them then worked tirelessly to recruit from the community, calling on their own networks and advertising the programme in shops, nurseries and the mosque. They urged women to show the leaflet to their families. The tutors had asked if we could offer some form of accreditation, explaining that access to the mainstream culture was generally perceived in terms of the necessity for 'proof' of academic/skills ability. I rehearsed the 'accreditation debate' once again but the tutors pointed out that without some form of palpable 'outcome', any women who wished to attend would find it difficult to persuade their families of the usefulness of the course. They asked if we might offer a certificate of attendance which could list the skills included during the class sessions. I agreed to this, albeit reluctantly. No doubt the skills elements would be included but what value would the certificate have in the eyes of prospective employers? I was also concerned that the students might be misled into assuming that the certificate amounted to a passport to a job and urged the tutors to be wary of issuing false promises. I was becoming increasingly aware of a widening gap between our initial educational intentions – 'this course is a good thing' – and the perceptions of our intended 'target group'.

There were initially 10 women on the course. One of them left for family reasons, the others returned twice a week for the next seven weeks. The following extracts are taken from our initial advertising and the tutors' own accounts of the process:

Learn how to help yourself to recognise the skills and knowledge your experiences have given you.

This course includes:

- help with job applications and interviews

- study skills and group work

- certificate of attendance and skills gained

Most of the students had a good general knowledge and a wide variety of skills to share with their colleagues ... As most of them had gone through similar experiences of life at one stage or another, it helped form a special relationship within the group ... In the class, all the students were very eager to learn and achieve, which I felt made it easy for everyone to settle down and get on with their work; helping each other which, in turn, made it easy for me to teach because all the students showed and shared respect for everyone in the class.

I asked the students what they thought about this course. In their own words: 'Attending MEC has proved very beneficial and worthwhile for us. We feel more confident now. We have learnt to recognise our skills' ... They said they have learnt many words, spellings and making sentences in the MEC course. This is in addition to their prior knowledge, but they feel they need more and to get better equipped to seek employment.

Two of the students are entering further education in the autumn term; another has found employment. Two others are considering leaving their current employment and seeking re-training.

All the students would like to attend a similar course in the near future because they feel they have taken the first step to help themselves and would like to carry on and achieve, feeling independent and aware of their abilities.

On the last day of the course we held a celebration. The representative from the TEC came to award the certificates of attendance and the local paper recorded the event with a picture and an article stating that:

Immigrant Punjabi-speaking women have graduated from a course which aims to help them get a job. The Make Experience Count course teaches them to explain their life and work experiences in India to prospective employers in Britain (Gravesend Reporter, *August 4, 1994).*

All of the women have asked for a 'follow-on' course because they feel that they have only begun to explore the opportunities available to them. We have asked the TEC for more money. As I write, I am waiting for their response. It would be a pity if the words of the tutor on the training programme who left were to hold true, and our provison were to disappear after only a few weeks of 'outreach'. I stated at the beginning of this chapter that the course had proved a great success. The tutors and the students spoke of its value and of the importance of having a space in which to learn new skills, share anxieties and seek and provide mutual encouragement and support. One of the tutors concluded her report with the following:

> It is my belief that in future the course should be open to all women irrespective of ethnic origin. All women who are unemployed are disadvantaged and would benefit greatly from this course. To present the course as for Punjabi women only restricts the number of students and could lead to resentment in other groups. However, there should still be advertising in Punjabi and encouragement of attendance from the Punjabi community through the outreach workers. Where practical, tailored advertising should also be developed for other ethnic minorities. I recognise that this is a difficult issue and that other views are also justifiable. Overall this was a highly successful course, and highly valued by the students. It would be excellent if we could run this course again.

My colleagues and I shall endeavour to find the funds to do so, but if they are not forthcoming to what extent will the success of this project, as far as the students are concerned, outweigh our failure to meet the women's newly-articulated needs and expectations?

Conclusions

And what is the shape of my story, the story my time tells me to tell? Perhaps it is the avoidance of a single shape that tells the tale ... (Hoffman, 1989).

It is customary at the end of a book to write a conclusion; to offer a summary of the issues raised, to make explicit the lessons learned and thence effect a satisfactory closure. This tradition is in keeping with the requirements of the classic narrative. The reader has embarked upon a journey and assumes that a destination will have been reached at the turn of the last page. This journey thus mirrors our expectations of life. We have experienced a process, reflected upon it and emerged at the end with a keener apprehension of the effects it has wrought.

Yet I stated at the outset that this is a journey without a destination, that the 'reader, as fellow traveller, will speculate on the far-flung horizons according to her own lights and experiences'. But something is expected, and so I shall adhere to the contract as far as recapitulating the issues. The rest is up to you.

This book has highlighted some of the crucial questions that have arisen in our work with Making Experience Count courses in the WEA South Eastern District. It has touched upon the concerns, contradictions and dilemmas pertaining to certain current paradigmatic shifts within our definitions of, and practices within, the educational field. It has noted the faultline separating the liberal and vocational terrain and has emphasised the dangers inherent in adhering to individual empowerment at the expense of social change.

It has asked whether there is a distinction to be made between APL and APEL, and acknowledged that an early belief in the value of *experiential* learning might have been simplistic because the process begged three basic questions. It assumed:

- the concept of a unified subject enjoying equality of opportunity
- experience to be coherent, consistent and a site for rational intellectual excavation
- parity between learning gained in one arena and the skills and competences demanded by another.

The book described the contradictions that arose when facilitating a range of Making Experience Count courses within the WEA South Eastern District and illustrated that contradiction by not knowing whether to place MEC within or without the usual definitions of APEL.

The book repeated its concern with the relationship between individual and collective empowerment. It highlighted the problems that ensue when facilitating a personally reflective process within a hierarchical and public arena. It urged the need for a collective approach to learning whilst acknowledging the difficulties in that approach for a group of individuals for whom connection to others had been the major source of conflict.

The book looked to the specific needs of women and formulated a learning programme which took issue with the implicit 'male-centred' approach of most adult learning theory. Yet, in positing a 'gynagogic' antidote to the 'andragogic' model, the book acknowledged the difficulties inherent in postulating any theory which subsumes class, ethnic, sexual and group difference within a single, homogeneous category.

The book has pointed to the fragile distinctions between our categories of 'unwaged', 'part-time' and 'full-time' workers. It extended the theme by referring elsewhere to the divisive habit of describing 'students' or 'adult partakers of educational programmes' as if these people were in some way different from 'ourselves', the people who write papers and books about them.

The book also lamented the reductionism intrinsic to much educational practice whilst, within its own pages, describing a project designed to translate MEC to a different cultural context – for whose ultimate benefit?

In the midst of these contradictions, and to speak in its favour, the book also urged a greater awareness of the roles and responsibilities of the 'educator' and declared that 'educational responsibility lies in providing for dissonance and disagreement'. If it has achieved that, at least, then this 'time to reflect' has been worthwhile.

Bibliography

Belenky, M., Clinchy, B., Goldberger, N. and Tarule, J. (1986) *Women's Ways of Knowing. The Development of self, voice and mind*, Basic Books.

Bloom, B.S. *et al.* (1956) *Taxonomy of Educational Objectives. 1: The cognitive domain*, Longman, Green and Co.

Boud, D., Cohen, R. and Walker, D. (eds) (1993) *Using Experience for Learning*, Society for Research into Higher Education and Open University Press.

Brew, A. (1993) 'Unlearning through experience', in Boud *et al.* (1993).

Brown, R. *et al.* (1995) *The Profile Pack*, Macmillan.

Buckle, J. (1988) *A Learner's Introduction to Building on Your Experience*, The Learning From Experience Trust.

Butler, L. (1993) 'Unpaid work in the home and accreditation', in Thorpe *et al.* (1993).

Crawford, J., Kippax, S., Onyx, J., Gault, U. and Benton, P. (1992) *Emotion and Gender: Constructing meaning from memory*, Sage.

Daines, J. (1994) *Learning Outcomes in the WEA: Towards a description. A research report*, The Department of Adult Education, University of Nottingham.

Davenport, J. (1987) 'Is there any way out of the andragogy morass?', in Thorpe *et al.* (1993).

de Ville, J., Crowhurst, G. and Hull, C. (1991) *The Learning Manual*, Department of Continuing and Community Education, Goldsmiths' College, University of London.

Dewey, J. (1963) *Experience and Education*, Macmillan.

Edwards, R., Sieminski, S., and Zeldin, D. (eds) (1993) *Adult Learners, Education and Training*, Routledge.

Evans, N. (1988) 'The Assessment of Prior Experiential Learning. Report of a CNAA Development Fund project conducted at The Learning From Experience Trust', CNAA Development Services Publication no 17.

Field, J. (1991) 'Out of the adult hut: institutionalization, individuality and new values in the education of adults', in Raggat and Unwin (1991).

Firth, A. (1991) *Goldsmiths' College: A centenary account*, The Athlone Press.

Fraser, W. (1993) 'Learner Managed Learning in an Institution of Higher Education', Goldsmiths' College, University of London.

Gunew, S. (ed.) (1990) *Feminist Knowledge: Critique and construct*, Routledge.

Henriques, J., Holloway, W., Urwin, C., Venn, C. and Walkerdine, V. (1984) *Changing the Subject: Psychology, social regulation and subjectivity*, Methuen.

Hoffman, E. (1989) *Lost in Translation: A life in a new language*, Heinemann.

Hopson, B. and Scally, M. (1991) *Build Your Own Rainbow: A workbook for career and life management*, Mercury.

Hull, C. (1992) 'Making experience count: facilitating the APEL process', in Mulligan and Griffin (1992).

Humm, M. (1989) 'Subjects in English: autobiography, women and education', in Thompson, A. and Wilcox, H. (eds) (1989) *Teaching Women. Feminism and English studies*, Manchester University Press.

Jarvis, P. (1985) *The Sociology of Adult and Continuing Education*, Routledge.

Keep, E. (1993) 'Missing, presumed skilled: training policy in the UK', in Edwards *et al.* (1993).

Knowles, M. (1980) *The Modern Practice of Adult Education: From pedagogy to andragogy*, Chicago: Follet.

Kolb, D. (1984) 'The process of experiential learning', in Thorpe *et al.* (1993).

Kolb, D. and Fry, R. (1975) 'Towards an applied theory of experiential learning', in Cooper, C.L. (ed.) (1975) *Theories of Group Processes*, Wiley.

Lambert, P. (1987) *Assessing Prior Learning: Progress and practice*, FEU.

Lea, M. and West, L. (1994a) 'Identity, the adult learner and institutional change', in Armstrong, P. *et al.* (eds) (1994) *Reflecting on Changing Practices, Contexts and Identities*, SCUTREA Conference Proceedings, July 1994.

Lea, M. and West, L. (1994b) 'Telling stories: transition, self narratives and the struggle for meaning among adults in HE', in Papers from the 13th Annual Canadian Association for the Study of Adult Education Theory and Practice Conference, 1994.

Levinson, D. (1978) *The Seasons of a Man's Life*, Ballantyne.

Make Your Experience Count. A pack for group leaders. P 987 Community Education. The Open University. Produced in association with Somerset Education Services.

McGivney, V. (1990) *Education's for Other People: Access to education for non-participant adults*, NIACE.

McLean, S. (1980) *Female Circumcision, Excision and Infibulation: The facts and a proposal for change*, Minority Rights Group, no 47.

Mulligan, J. and Griffin, C. (eds) (1992) *Empowerment through Experiential Learning. Explorations of good practice*, Kogan Page.

Norquay, N. (1990) 'Life history research: memory, schooling and social difference', *Cambridge Journal of Education*, vol. 20, no. 3.

Oakley, A. (1981) *Subject Women*, Fontana.

Raggat, P. and Unwin, L. (eds) (1991) *Change and Intervention: Vocational education and training*, The Falmer Press.

Rajan, A. (1991) 'The case for targets', in *National Targets for Education and Training*, HMSO.

Ramazanoglu, C. (1989) *Feminisms and the Contradictions of Oppression*, Routledge.

Rothfield, P. (1990) 'Feminism, subjectivity, and sexual difference', in Gunew (1990)

Sheehy, G. (1974) *Passages*, E.P. Dutton.

Tawney, R.H. (1953) *The Workers' Educational Association and Adult Education*, The Athlone Press.

Tennant, M. (1988) 'Adult development', in Thorpe *et al.* (1993)

Thorpe, M., Edwards, R. and Hanson, A. (eds) (1993) *Culture and Processes of Adult Learning*, Routledge.

Usher, R. (1985) 'Beyond the anecdotal: adult learning and the use of experience', *Studies in the Education of Adults*, vol. 17, no. 1.

Usher, R. (1989) 'Qualifications, paradigms and experiential learning in HE', in Fulton, O. (ed.) (1989) *Access and Institutional Change*, Society for Research into Higher Education and Open University Press.

Usher, R. (1993) 'Experiential learning or learning from experience: does it make a difference?', in Boud *et al.* (1993).

Warner Weil, S. (1989) 'Access: towards education or miseducation? Adults imagine the future', in Thorpe *et al.* (1993).

Warner Weil, S. and McGill, I. (eds) (1989) *Making Sense of Experiential Learning. Diversity in theory and practice*, Society for Research into Higher Education and Open University Press.

Workers' Educational Association *1918 Yearbook*.

Workers' Educational Association *1919 Report*.

Workers' Educational Association *Getting Started*.

Workers' Educational Association (1989) *Women's Education Past, Present and Future: Policy Statement*.

West, L. (1995) 'Beyond fragments: adults, motivation and higher education', *Studies in the Education of Adults*, vol. 27, no. 2.

West, L. and Fraser, W. (1992) 'The Assessment of Prior Experiential Learning in Universities' Admissions Procedures', University of Kent.
Woodley, A. *et al.* (1987) *Choosing to Learn: Adults in education*, Society for Research into Higher Education and Open University Press.

Handout References

Handout 1: *Resource Materials for the Assessment of Experiential Learning*, The Learning From Experience Trust (LET) in association with the County of Avon Education Department (hereafter referred to as CAED), 1987, p.26.
Handout 2: *Handbook for the Assessment of Experiential Learning*, LET with CAED, 1987, p.6.
Handout 3: *ibid.*, p.11.
Handout 4: *ibid.*, p.13.
Handout 5: *Resource Materials for the Assessment of Experiential Learning*, pp27–30.
Handout 6: *A Learner's Introduction to Building on Your Experience*, Buckle, J., LET, 1988, p.8.
Handout 7: *ibid.*, pp24–25.
Handout 8: *Handbook for the Assessment of Experiential Learning*, p.18.
Handout 9: *ibid.*, p.24.
Handout 10: *A Learner's Introduction to Building on Your Experience*, pp31–36.